ANNE ARNOTT

Valiant for TRUTH

The Story of John Bunyan

Foreword by Stuart Blanch

WM. B. EERDMANS PUBLISHING CO.
Grand Rapids, Michigan

Copyright © 1985 by Anne Arnott

First published 1985 under the title *He Shall with Giants Fight*
by Kingsway Publications Ltd., Lottbridge Drove,
Eastbourne, East Sussex BN23 6NT, England.
Illustrations by Brian Tutt

This edition published 1986 through special arrangement with Kingsway by
Wm. B. Eerdmans Publishing Co., 255 Jefferson Ave. SE, Grand Rapids, Mich. 49503

Printed in the United States of America

Library of Congress Cataloging-in-Publication Data

Arnott, Anne.
Valiant for truth.

Previously published as: He shall with giants fight.
Bibliography: p. 158
1. Bunyan, John, 1626-1688 — Biography.   2. Authors.
English — Early modern, 1500-1700 — Biography.
3. Puritans — England — Clergy — Biography.   I. Title.
PR3331.A76   1986   828′.407 [B]   86-16518

ISBN 0-8028-0192-7

Contents

'Tell them that they have left their house and home,
Are turned Pilgrims, seek a world to come.'

Pilgrim's Progress (Part II)

Foreword

This is a good, well-organized account of one of the great figures of the Reformation, a valiant fighter for truth, a preacher and a pastor, and the author of one of the best-selling books in the history of English literature. *The Pilgrim's Progress* has been translated into many languages and often quoted even when the source of the quotation is unknown. But what of the man himself, whose book had so great an influence on English life and literature?

John Bunyan's father was a tinker, and he followed in his father's trade. He was, of necessity, a man of limited education, but endowed with a powerful mind and a glittering imagination. He was a man of no consequence, so it seemed, yet achieved undying fame. He was a man who combined great powers of public utterance with a painful experience of doubt and spiritual struggle. The giants with whom he fought were not just the powerful establishment figures of his day, but the powerful enemies within. He deserves a good popular biography and the author has provided just that.

Anne Arnott has not only explored the heights and depths of Bunyan's inner life; she has set him firmly within the context of seventeenth-century politics and theology. In her admiration for her subject she does not conceal from the reader the strangeness of his mental scenery and occasionally quixotic character. He was a man of his time, as much part of his world as we are inescapably part of ours. The reader will have to learn to live with a view of life which will seem to some as remote as the Flood. But John Bunyan had something important to say, in life and word, and he needs to be heard in our own day, with our easy-going view of great religious and moral issues, our superficial, hedonistic attitudes to life, with our seeming indifference to truth. Bunyan was a man valiant for truth; he spoke of it, he gave his life for it, he suffered for it, he spent desolating years in prison rather than betray it. He deserves to be heard and Anne Arnott has helped to make him audible to our generation.

With this book in hand we will learn something we all need to learn, not only about John Bunyan but about the mighty issues with which he was concerned, and the grandeur of the faith for which he suffered. The trumpet that sounded for him on the other side, reverberates still on this side of the grave, and will continue to do so wherever men continue to honour integrity, courage and faith.

STUART BLANCH

The Prisoner

In the sombre day-room of Bedford County Gaol in the year 1666, a man was sitting at a small table under a high barred window. In front of him was a tall candlestick, an open book and a pen. He was deep in thought, and his eyes seemed to be looking into some distant place far beyond the gloom of his surroundings. He had a strong face and looked like a countryman with his fresh complexion and reddish hair. He wore the dark plain jacket and breeches of a Puritan.

The gloomy room around him was crowded and stuffy; all sorts and conditions of men and women—some ragged, others neatly dressed—were sitting and standing about, jostling together. Some were talking, some shouting across the room, and a few weeping. A small group, also in Puritan dress, were clustered together in a corner with Bibles in their hands, which they were reading together in low voices. They were Nonconformist ministers, turned out of their livings, and arrested for preaching at meetings held outside the Established Church of England. For England was experiencing the aftermath of the Civil War, Cromwell was dead, and Charles II was on the throne.

Outside, the clocks of Bedford chimed the slowly passing hours, but the prisoner who sat quietly at the table barely heard them. In his imagination he was on a perilous journey. A great drama was unfolding in his mind. He could not then have dreamed that his words would be read by thousands throughout England, and would be translated into many languages across the world; nor that his book would be a timeless masterpiece, still read today over three hundred years later, and as fresh and alive now as it was when first written.

A great drama was unfolding in his mind (page 10).

CHAPTER 1

The Boy

1628 was a turbulent year. It saw the opening of Charles I's Third Parliament, and the feeling of some members ran so high at the King's apparently careless violation of Parliamentary rights that some, it is recorded, were actually in tears. The seeds of civil war were being sown, and there was restlessness and discontent in many places.

Far away from these conflicts and the affairs of state, a baby, John, was born in this year to Thomas and Mary Bunyan in a cottage in the little hamlet of Harrowden at the eastern end of the village of Elstow, one mile south of Bedford. John's grandfather owned the cottage, which had belonged to the family for generations. It stood at the foot of a gently sloping hill between two streams at a place called Bunyan's End. He was a chapman who carried small goods to sell from village to village. Among these were chapbooks which contained popular ballads, legends and old romances, such as 'Sir Bevis of Southampton' and 'George on Horseback'.

John's father, Thomas, was a brazier or tinker, not a travelling gypsy or vagrant, but a man with a recognized and honourable trade, 'a mender of pots and kettles', as he was described. He would travel from his home to the surrounding villages and farms to get work wherever he could. He would then work at his forge beside the cottage, repairing the utensils, and farm implements and harness too. He also helped to cultivate the few acres around the cottage. Little is known about him except that he married his first wife when he was barely twenty, and she died after four years, when he married John's mother, Margaret Bentley.

The only picture of what sort of man he was comes in a chance description of him by Thomas Archer, Rector of Houghton Conquest, the parish next to Elstow. He kept a diary of his life in the country and of little events of interest. One day he notes this unusual little piece of natural history:

> Memorandum—That in Anno 1625 one Bonion of Elsto clyminge of Rookes neasts in the Bery wood ffound 3 Rookes in a nest, all white as milke and not a blacke fether on them.

As rook's nests are always very high in the tallest trees, this picture suggests an athletic vigorous young man; to reach a nest would be a tremendous feat of climbing, unless it had fallen to lower branches in a gale.

John's mother, Margaret Bentley, must have known Thomas Bunyan all her life as she, too, belonged to Elstow. We know that her mother was a good-living woman who, four years after the baby's birth left a legacy in her will to her daughter—one of six children—which read, 'I give to my daughter Margaret the joined stoole in the chamber and my little case.' This suggests that there was not much to leave; but nevertheless really poverty-stricken people of the time never left wills.

Later there were wills made by John's grandfather and father, and this too indicates that the family were certainly not among the poorest of the poor.

The cottage home at Harrowden would have a thatched roof and wattle and daub walls. Beside it would be a barn and stable and a yard. Herbs and vegetables would be grown in the small garden. Cottages generally had also a small orchard and an enclosed pasture, for those who lived in them had to be self-sufficient. So as well as some wheat barley or rye, flax and hemp were cultivated for weaving clothing. Livestock would include chickens, a few sheep, a pig or two, a horse, a cow, and some bees which would provide the only sugar for the house. Inside the cottage, the wooden furniture, often home-made, would be strong and simple. Pewter and brass pots were essential kitchen utensils and prized by the housewife.

Into such a home John Bunyan was born. In November, 1628, he was carried across the village green to Elstow Church to be baptized. No one on that day could possibly have imagined what his future was to hold.

When John Bunyan wrote briefly about his parents and home many years later, he gives a rather worse picture than might be expected:

> For my descent then, it was, as is well known by many, of a low and inconsiderable generation, my father's house being of the rank that is meanest and most despised of all families in the land.

Indeed, he seems particularly sensitive about his parents' poverty, and the times may well have been very hard for the family. But a contemporary of Bunyan describes his father as 'an honest poor labouring man, who, like Adam unparadised, had all the world to get his bread in, and was very careful to maintain his family.'

In later years John Bunyan describes how, as he grew to boyhood, one advantage was given him that was certainly not given to all the poor boys of his day: he was sent to school. It seems likely that he showed signs of an unusually lively intelligence and a very vivid imagination, and that he was exceedingly active and fond of all play and sport. Perhaps his parents, recognizing something special about their first child, wanted to give him every advantage. Bunyan later described their efforts on his behalf:

But yet, notwithstanding the meanness and inconsiderableness of my parents, it pleased God to put it into their hearts to put me to school to learn both to read and write, the which I also attained according to the rate of other poor men's children.

The school which he probably attended was Sir William Harper's Grammar School in Bedford, founded exclusively 'for nourishing and educating poor boys in that place'. If this is correct, it is small wonder that the little he learned he soon forgot 'almost utterly' as he confessed. For when John Bunyan was about nine or ten, a petition complaining about the schoolmaster, William Varney, was sent to the House of Lords, stating that he had not only charged fees which he had no right to do, but had 'grossly neglected the school by frequent absence from it, by night-walking and mis-spending his time in taverns and ale-houses, and is also very cruel when present to the boys'.

Bunyan, who wrote that he never learned classics, like Aristotle or Plato, as sons of wealthier boys did, was before long called home from school to help his father at the forge. As he was a boy who loved to go out and play with his friends, it may have been hard to join the working men, and he recalled that he was then 'brought up in a very mean condition among the company of poor countrymen'.

By now he had a sister, Margaret, a year younger than himself, and a brother William, some years younger, and as the eldest child he may well have had to help his mother when his father was away travelling to the villages around. Sometimes he may also have gone with his father to the cottages of the yeomen and craftsmen and to the small farms in the country around, or even to the great mansion Houghton House on nearby Ampthill hill, whose old account books have an entry of the time, 'paid the brazier'. There is no doubt that he would have loved to hear the old tales from his grandfather's chapbooks; and when he could be freed from helping his father, he enjoyed nothing better than joining the village boys to play tipcat and other games on Elstow green.

When, years later, John Bunyan wrote *Grace Abounding to the Chief of Sinners,* which tells of his own spiritual journey, various sidelights on his complex character clearly emerge. He describes how, as a boy, he had terrible dreams. He lived at a time when people's thoughts dwelt on the supernatural, when there was a strong belief in witchcraft, and it was common to talk about it. But he was exceptionally imaginative, and the fear of evil seemed to possess him. He dreamed of devils and evil spirits, and felt, he said, that they 'laboured to draw me away with them'. This caused him acute fear and distress.

If the fears crowded in at night, he would compensate by flinging himself into all sorts of sports by day, trying to forget. But even then the shadow of the terror he had experienced would creep over him and he would become very depressed, even at play:

> These things, I say, when I was but a child but nine or ten years old, did so distress my soul, that then, in the midst of my many sports and childish vanities, amidst my vain companions I was often much cast down, and afflicted in my mind therewith.

There was also a daring, wild and often merry side to his character. He was a ringleader, loving all adventure, all games, music and, above all, dancing. As a boy he would watch the Morris dancers, their bells jingling around their knees, and he would join in the dances on the village green with the other villagers. He gives the impression of having great vitality.

In *Grace Abounding* he describes very briefly three incidents in his life which suggested to him when he looked back on them that even then God must have been watching over him and protecting him. He describes how he was boating in a creek by the sea, and fell into the water and only narrowly escaped drowning. He also fell out of a boat into 'Bedford river' (the Ouse), 'But mercy,' he said, 'yet

preserved me.' The third incident was when he found an
adder on the road. He struck it and stunned it, and then
with foolish bravado forced open its mouth and pulled out
what he thought was the sting, presumably the tongue.
Ashamed of this years later he wrote, 'By which act, had
God not been merciful unto me, I might by my desperate-
ness have brought myself to my end.'

As John Bunyan grew into a teenage boy, his violent
temper was prone to flare up. He constantly cursed and
swore and used much bad language—something he was
bitterly sorry about in later years. He began to feel he
served the devil, who was so terrifyingly real to him. He
wrote: 'I had but few equals for cursing, swearing, lying
and blaspheming the holy name of God.'

Somehow he was always at war with himself, and there
was a battle in his mind between good and evil. He describes how he used to study people almost wistfully,
especially when he felt they were really good people, to
see if their goodness was true and consistent. There was
this desire to see the highest standards in others. It was a
search for perfection of character in those whom he
admired. But he was deeply depressed if those whom he
judged to be really good, turned out not to be so. He
wrote:

> If I had at any time seen wicked things, by those who professed
> goodness, it would make my spirit tremble.

Knowing how often he himself swore, he yet confessed
that, 'Hearing one to swear that was reckoned for a religious man, it had so great a stroke upon my spirit that it
made my heart ache.' Clearly he was vulnerable, looking
for the good, watching out for the integrity in people, and
becoming disillusioned when he did not find it.

The time came when life changed for the worse, bringing
him tragedy. It seems likely that John Bunyan really loved
his mother—this is suggested by his pen pictures of good

women in all he wrote years later. It may be that he was a great helper to her when his father was constantly travelling from place to place to get work. She may have been overworked, perhaps anxious as to how to make ends meet, particularly when she had three young children. We do not know if any other children had died in infancy, as so often happened at the time. Illness could be a serious and dreaded matter. Medicine in the country usually consisted of homely remedies, with herbs being used in various potions, knowledge of which was passed down from mother to daughter, and, in fact, there was real value in some of these simple remedies. Yet disease and infections often spread with fatal rapidity.

We do not know what actually happened, but when John was sixteen, his mother died. She was carried across to the quiet churchyard at Elstow for burial. A month later, his sister Margaret died also.

What then happened is not known, and can only be guessed. What is recorded is that John's father, probably shattered by the double loss, with two motherless boys, the younger only eleven, and with a job that took him travelling away from home, knew he could not manage. With what must have seemed shocking haste to the boys, he married again before a month had passed. Perhaps it was a marriage of convenience in a desperate situation. What does seem clear is that John Bunyan was deeply affected. A hatred of all religion seized him. God seemed to have deserted the family. In bitter words he was much later to record his feelings:

> In those days the thoughts of religion were very grievous to me; I could neither endure it myself, nor that any other should; so that when I have seen some read in those books that concerned Christian piety, it would be as it were a prison to me. Then I said unto God, 'Depart from me, for I desire not the knowledge of thy ways.'

Restless and sick at heart, he eventually found a way of escape. He left home and joined Cromwell's army to fight in the Civil War. He was sixteen.

CHAPTER 2

The Soldier

John Bunyan was growing into a man in times of ferment and conflict in England.

During 1642 both Royalists and Parliamentarians were actively raising troops. The great strength of the Parliament's support was in London, and the London 'trained bands' protected the Puritan leaders while the king was gathering his army in the north. All hopes of reconciliation between King and Parliament steadily faded.

In the late summer of 1642, the king raised his standard at Nottingham. War had begun. It was a sad and desperate time. Although some of the young Royalist officers were eager to fight, there was a sombre mood among most men at the prospect of fighting against their own countrymen in a war which would even divide members of a family. One Puritan gentleman on the Parliament's side wrote to a Royalist friend:

> The great God, who is the searcher of my heart, knows with what reluctance I go upon this service, and with what perfect hatred I look upon war without an enemy. We are both on the stage, and we must act the parts assigned to us in this tragedy; let us do it in a way of honour, without personal animosities.

A great Royalist, Sir Edmund Verney, sorrowfully expressed a Royalist's feeling:

I have eaten the king's bread and served him over thirty years, and I will not do so base a thing as to forsake him.

It was after the indecisive battle of Edgehill in 1642 and the various campaigns of 1643 that the king's forces were checked as they advanced into Lincolnshire. The Puritan armies of East Anglia, which was strong for Parliament, had been organized into the Eastern Association, and were kept together by the brilliant organization of the Huntingdon Squire—one of the only great leaders of the war—Oliver Cromwell. The discipline of his famous troops was excellent. No gambling or swearing, no drunkenness, and no plundering were allowed in his army. The king held most of England, but Parliament drew much of its strength from East Anglia and the Home Counties around London, including Bedfordshire.

The military leader in Bedfordshire was Sir Samuel Luke of Cople Wood End, one of the Members of Parliament for Bedford in the Long Parliament before the War. He was the governor of the garrison at Newport Pagnell. Letters he wrote at the time indicate that he was a broad-minded humane man of great courage. Not only was he a man of keen observation who had a strong sense of humour, but he was a God-fearing man. He was not at all like the traditional but often erroneous idea of a Puritan as narrow-minded and bigoted. Strangely enough, there was a small link between him and the Bunyan family. His confidential servant was Edward Bynion (the name is spelt in various ways in documents) who was John Bunyan's uncle, his father's brother. Moreover this Edward was doubly a relative, for he was married to John's mother's sister, Rose.

In 1643 Sir Samuel Luke issued a proclamation that was fastened up in the villages of South Bedfordshire in July, 1643. This called on every boy and man between sixteen and twenty to carry arms for Parliament and to appear 'at Leighton on Monday morning by seven of the clock, with

all provisions with them, and arms and weapons for the
service of the State and their own safety....' In due time
this proclamation would have reached Elstow.

So, by the autumn of 1644, a very excited John Bunyan
had left home to become a foot soldier in Cromwell's New
Model Army, probably under Sir Samuel Luke. Bunyan's
name has been found on the muster roll of the Parliamentary Army at Newport Pagnell. He now found himself
among men of an entirely different sort from those among
whom he had grown up. Many were 'the preaching cap-
tains and praying privates', the Puritans of the New Model
Army. Perhaps, seeing them, thoughts came to him of a
better life than he had lived at home. He watched and
noted all that went on. He thrilled to the sight of thousands
of troops being trained, of men advancing to lay siege to a
town. The discipline, the comradeship, the outdoor life
all gripped him, and in one way he became a soldier at
heart for the rest of his life. But years later he would be
fighting in a very different kind of war.

When, in middle life, he came to write his second great
allegorical tale, *The Holy War*, he gave it a setting which
came straight out of his own experience in the Civil War.
Here are pictured the military exercises of the army of
Shaddai, marching and counter-marching, turning and
wheeling; here is the training in arms, all reminiscent of
Cromwell's army. The recollection still had the power to
stir and excite him:

> They marched, they counter-marched, they opened to the
> right and left, they divided and sub-divided, they closed,
> they wheeled, made good their front and rear with their
> right and left wings, and twenty things more, with that
> aptness, and then they were all as they were again, that
> they took, yea, ravished the hearts that were in Mansoul to
> behold it.

In the introductory verses to the book he draws vivid

pictures of troops coming to besiege a town—it is believed he was at the siege of Leicester—and he conveys his own excitement and feeling of tension at the time of battle:

> I saw the Prince's armed men come down
> By troops, by thousands, to besiege the town;
> I saw the captains, heard the trumpets sound,
> And how his forces covered all the ground.
> Yea, how they set themselves in battle-'ray,
> I shall remember to my dying day.

John Bunyan only records one incident from his army days. He describes in *Grace Abounding* how he had yet another narrow escape from death. That he was saved by an apparent coincidence seemed to him in retrospect nothing less than the hand of God:

> This also I have taken notice of with thanksgiving: When I was a soldier, I with others, were drawn out to go to such a place to besiege it; but when I was just ready to go, one of the company desired to go in my room; to which when I had consented, he took my place; and coming to the siege, as he stood sentinel, he was shot in the head with a musket-ball, and died.

As he looked back at those days, he describes himself as a boy, barely grown to manhood, still angry and rebellious, with no purpose in life:

> Here, as I said, were judgments and mercy, but neither of them did awaken my soul to righteousness; wherefore I sinned still, and grew more and more rebellious against God, and careless of my own salvation.

No one then could possibly have foreseen that through much trial and hardship he would one day become a disciplined soldier of brilliant gifts and immense courage in the army of the Lord.

History

CHAPTER 3

A Conflict of Minds

John Bunyan left the army to go back to Elstow utterly unaware of the dynamic change that, before long, would alter his whole life. He had undoubtedly found army life exciting. He was a village boy from a poor family who had not travelled far before. Now he had met men of all sorts and conditions, had stood beside many Puritans in the army, and had almost certainly listened to some of the officers preaching strong biblical sermons when the army was in camp, or garrisoned at Newport Pagnell. He had heard men praying fervently before battle and had watched their grim determination. He had thrilled to the banners, the trumpets, the marching of hundreds of men, and had probably felt part of a great cause, although it was the political aspect of fighting for justice, rather than any religious aim which would then have gripped him. In Cromwell's New Model Army the principle of equality was uppermost, and he no doubt heard the arguments for all men to have equal rights in elections for Parliament, and to have just shares in the ownership of land. He may well have been impressed by the fervour with which the Puritans held their views and their faith, even if he pretended it meant little to him.

But who exactly were the Puritans, those soberly dressed men and women who were thought of as kill-joys by many, and were mocked at for not taking part in dancing, theatre-going, Sunday sport and much else? John Bunyan may well, like others, have regarded them as stern and narrow-minded, opposed to all amusements. Yet such a picture was at least in part, inaccurate and unjust.

To discover who they were, it is necessary to take a journey back in time. Like detectives, we must gather and select information and piece together historical events and developments until we see the different influences that moulded their thinking over the years. The result was a faith so powerful that it captivated people's hearts and minds. This was a faith they were determined to defend at all costs; it was a faith that one day would inspire the heart of John Bunyan.

For over a hundred years before the birth of John Bunyan there had been a growing ferment of thought, a revolution in men's minds. It had erupted in 1517 when the German monk, Martin Luther, the great scholar and reformer of Wittenberg, challenged the authority of the Roman Catholic Church, which was virtually universal in most of Europe. After intense study of the Bible, he attacked the wealth and corruption of the Roman Church, particularly the enormous sale of Indulgences—papers with the pope's signature on them promising that whoever bought them would spend less time being punished in purgatory after death. All the money people paid out for Indulgences went to the church. Luther believed most strongly and openly stated that we go to heaven only by trusting Jesus Christ. We cannot work our own way into heaven, or buy our way there. He attacked the supremacy of the pope, and contrasted the treasures of the church with its true wealth, the gospel of Jesus Christ.

Luther refused to recant, and worked to reform public worship. He stressed the preaching of the Bible, the communion, and congregational singing. To this day his great hymn 'A safe stronghold our God is still' is heard in many churches.

Luther's famous words when told to recant ring down the centuries:

> I stand convicted by the Scriptures to which I have appealed, and my conscience is taken captive by God's Word. I cannot and will not recant anything. For to act against our conscience is neither safe for us, nor open to us. On this I take my stand. I can do no other. God help me.

Luther's ideas were seized on eagerly by many in England, for there had been anti-papal feeling among some people for years. Now men began to think deeply for themselves instead of allowing the church to think for them. Luther's movement ultimately split Europe in two, and the Reformation began.

Luther had translated the New Testament into German so that it might be read by all. It was the great wish of the Reformers that the Bible, the word of God, might be made available to everyone in his own language, instead of being in Latin. In England, the pioneer of the translation of the English Bible was William Tyndale, who first published the New Testament in 1525, and also part of the Old Testament. Tyndale, a University of Oxford man and a tutor to the family of Sir William Walsh, had a great vision. He said to a clergyman 'If God spare my life, ere many years pass, I will cause a boy that driveth the plough shall know more of the Scriptures than thou dost.'

During the sixteenth century various translations of the Bible appeared. Many leading Protestants went into exile during the reign of the Roman Catholic Queen Mary, and those who went to Geneva determined to produce a new translation of the Bible. In 1560 the Geneva Bible appeared and became very popular in Britain, remaining so for fifty years after the appearance in 1611 of the Authorized Version, or King James' Bible, which is still widely used today. The Geneva Bible could be bought for a few shillings, and was to be found in a great number of homes. It was the Bible John Bunyan was to use years later.

Some years after Luther's great statement of faith, a young man in Paris, John Calvin, came across the teachings of Luther. Greatly struck by them, he experienced a remarkable sudden conversion in 1533. 'God subdued and brought my heart to docility,' he said. He, too, broke away from Roman Catholicism, studied deeply and formulated his beliefs, following in Luther's path. Through his writings, his commentaries on the Bible, and his preaching, he helped to consolidate the Reformation. He was a great reformer and tried to bring every citizen in Geneva, where he eventually lived and worked, under the moral discipline of the church. In this he was only partly successful. He founded the Geneva Academy to which students of theology came from all parts of western and central Europe. Like Luther, Calvin believed all knowledge of God and man is to be found in the Bible. But the church was of supreme importance to him, and he taught that it should not be restricted in any way by the state. He wanted a reformed Protestant church, free of much of the ritual of the Roman Catholic church, but laying great emphasis on the two sacraments of baptism and communion.

His ideas took hold of many people in England and Scotland and in England followers of his teaching eventually became known as Puritans, from their desire to purify the church.

This great ferment in religious thought had grown alongside and was inextricably mixed with dramatic political changes. In 1534 Henry VIII had declared himself Head of the Church of England after quarrelling with the pope who refused to sanction his divorce from Queen Catherine. During his reign Henry VIII destroyed the power of the pope in England, and put an end to monasticism. Thomas Cranmer became his Archbishop.

As a young man Cranmer had enthusiastically studied the teachings of Luther with Hugh Latimer and Nicholas Ridley, both of whom eventually became bishops, and these men led the Reformation forward in England. Cranmer was largely responsible for shaping the Protestant Church of England. In the short reign of Edward VI from 1547–1553 the Reformation was effectively introduced in England. But when Queen Mary, a most intolerant and bigoted Roman Catholic, came to the throne she attempted to restore Roman Catholicism. About two hundred bishops, scholars and other men and women, including the leaders of the reformation church, were burnt at the stake, including Archbishop Cranmer and the bishops Ridley and Latimer. They died with very great courage. Hugh Latimer, in his torture, cried out to Nicholas Ridley:

> Be of good comfort, Master Ridley, and play the man; we shall this day light such a candle by God's grace in England as I trust shall never be put out.

When Queen Elizabeth I came to the throne she permanently established Protestantism in England. But the strict Puritans within the church wanted to abolish all religious ceremonies and ritual on the grounds that they were remnants of Roman Catholicism. They did not want bishops, but church government by elders, and at first they had support in Parliament. But eventually this went too far for the Queen who called herself 'supreme governor' (not head) of the Church of England; and she kept the bishops. The liturgy, also, remained much as it is in the Prayer Book today, and the freer form of service the Puritans wanted was not allowed. Some Puritans then began to leave the Church of England and this movement away from the church continued in the reign of King James I who very vehemently opposed them. 'I will make them conform themselves or I will harry them out of the land, or else do worse,' he said. Some of these 'Separatists', who, for conscience sake, left the church, formed independent congregations; and for this some were imprisoned. Others fled the country, and very many settled in Holland, as the Dutch were very tolerant towards them.

The Puritans were mocked at in plays of the time. They were considered to be fanatics and were scorned and laughed at for refusing to take part in what they thought of as 'worldly' pleasures. In face of this, many behaved with great courage, enduring persecution without flinching. They were a body of people who were fighting to worship God simply. They believed they were worshipping God as he had been worshipped in the early church of the apostles and their faith meant everything to them. Their desire was not to take part in anything that might draw them away from God who had become so real to them through his word, the Bible. It is quite wrong to think they were grim unhappy people. In fact many were full of a quiet joy, a sort of inward serenity, because they profoundly believed they were called by God to recover something of the zeal and freshness and simplicity of the early Christians.

One of the bravest groups of Puritans was the 'Pilgrim Fathers' who, after exile in Holland, set out in 1620 for the New World and religious freedom. It was a hazardous journey into the unknown. About a hundred sailed from Plymouth in *The Mayflower*, facing great difficulties and dangers. A further group followed in 1628, the year when John Bunyan was born. Thousands more colonists were to follow between 1630 and 1643, and through these pioneers the American colonies were born.

Through the years of John Bunyan's boyhood, Puritanism was growing stronger, and by the time King Charles I came to the throne in 1625 a great body of people bitterly opposed his leanings towards Roman Catholicism, leanings which were the stronger because of his marriage to Henrietta Maria, herself a Roman Catholic and sister of the French King Louis XIII. Charles believed profoundly that kings governed by divine right. Although he was in many ways an attractive and charming man, his weakness and lack of wisdom, his continued opposition to Parliament and hostility to the Puritans aroused very deep resentment. King and Commons eventually clashed violently on financial matters, foreign affairs and religion. In 1629 Parliament condemned 'innovations in religion' and the 'introduction of popery'. Charles angrily retorted by declaring that the Commons had attempted 'to exert a universal, overswaying power, which belongs only to me and not to them'. He then ruled for eleven years without any Parliament. In 1633 he made the Bishop of London, William Laud, Archbishop of Canterbury. This move became fiercely unpopular. Laud was a very strict disciplinarian. He put down the Puritan separatist meetings outside the Church of England with great firmness, also fining many Puritan speakers and writers through his Court of High Commission. Indeed, he condemned what he saw as laxity anywhere, and not only amongst the Puritans, for example he punished a clergyman who dared to preach without a surplice, and an innkeeper who allowed drinking on Sunday. It was said of him that he did not know the meaning of toleration, and only saw things from his own point of view. As the Earl of Clarendon said, he could not 'debate anything without some commotion'.

By the time of the meeting of 'the Long Parliament' in 1640, the Commons were determined on reform. Hostility between King and Parliament increased violently, and soon the atmosphere was one of revolution which led to the Civil War.

After the war, however, the Commons over-reached themselves. The king's trial was a farce and a tragedy, and Charles reached his finest moments in his execution and death. As the poet Andrew Marvell wrote:

> He nothing common did or mean
> Upon that memorable scene.

The years after the Civil War, therefore, saw yet more violent change. And it was in those disturbed years that Bunyan, the boy soldier, went back to Elstow from the army to try and earn his living as best he could.

As in most villages, in many ways life probably went on much as usual with news from outside filtering in only gradually. This may well have made life seem dull to the young soldier. Everything went on as it had for decades, ruled by such events as the success or failure of the harvest, corn prices, village gossip, the family fortunes good or bad of village families, and by the excitement and boisterous gaiety of the village fairs that regularly enlivened country life. There was economic hardship, too, in the countryside in the 1640s, partly a result of the Civil War. But also the harvests of those years were poor, and food was often scarce. Work was hard to get, and many families faced great poverty.

Yet undoubtedly there was a new development in religious beliefs and practices among many ordinary people in town and village. At first the Puritans had come mainly from the middle classes with a few, like Cromwell, from the landed gentry and some from among the scholars and thinkers. But now the Puritans were increasingly found among tradesmen, shopkeepers and craftsmen, and among many who faced real poverty. The gospel teaching of the equal value of every soul before God was inspiring to those who felt themselves inferior, poor and underprivileged. Many travelling craftsmen were full of earnest zeal, and courageously preached the gospel of free salvation for all men through belief in Christ. These 'mechanic preachers' as they were called, preached on village greens, and in any open spaces where people gathered to listen. Bunyan, before many years had passed, was to be one of them. It was a gospel of hope, a declaration of the worth of every man, woman and child in the sight of God.

Many devout Roman Catholics, loyal to the pope, had suffered deeply too in those violent and troubled years. Sir Thomas More, great scholar and Chancellor in Henry VIII's reign, was one. An extraordinarily brave man, a faithful and dedicated Roman Catholic, he refused to agree to Henry's divorce from a totally innocent Queen, and to his marriage with Anne Boleyn with whom he was infatuated. For this he was eventually executed, as were a number of faithful priests, among others. During Elizabeth's reign, many Roman Catholic priests lived secretly in fear of their lives. Families who held to the 'old faith' retreated from public life. In many great houses they kept secret rooms or 'priest's holes', where priests could hide from of danger.

England was basically a religious country. Almost everyone went to church, and most people felt their loyalties lay in the Church of England. They accepted as right the government by bishops, and were content to use the Book of Common Prayer, many feeling sincerely that it contained all they needed for the practice of their faith. Others went to church purely in a nominal way, and church and the Christian faith were to them simply a natural and not closely questioned part of life.

The real tragedy of these long years lay in the fact that people everywhere utterly failed to understand each other, or to accept each person's right to worship as his conscience led him. The concept of toleration appeared to be meaningless.

CHAPTER 4

The Husband

John Bunyan was barely grown up when he came <u>home</u> <u>from the war</u>, and began to pick up the threads of his old life. He went back to Elstow, back to <u>his father's forge</u>, and to his work as a brazier, travelling from village to village and to the neighbouring town with his <u>iron anvil on</u> <u>his back</u>. Bearing the inscription J. Bunyan, Helstowe, <u>1647</u>, this anvil is still to be seen in the Bunyan Meeting House Museum at Bedford. John Bunyan's <u>job</u> was <u>making and mending household utensils of metal or pewter</u> <u>and farm implements</u>. He was <u>a craftsman</u> in a perfectly honourable trade, and when in later writing he describes himself as 'being of that rank that is meanest and most despised of the families in the Land', we would today say he was exaggerating. But in the days when he was writing his books, the Puritans considered it proper to describe their worldly position with <u>great</u> Christian <u>humility</u>, and other <u>writers of the time wrote in the same way</u>. But <u>poor</u> he certainly was, and it was probably hard at first to make a living.

On his journeys from village to village, strong though he must have been, his <u>sixty pound anvil</u> must have felt a <u>great burden</u>. Maybe this was in his mind when, years later, he wrote in *Pilgrim's Progress*:

I saw a man clothed with rags, standing in a certain place, with his face from his own house, a book in his hand, and a great burden on his back.

The words conjure up a feeling of sadness and hopelessness. But at this time he was to all appearances still the high-spirited and obviously popular leader of the village games and sport. Years later he wrote, 'Until I came to the state of marriage, I was the very ringleader of all the youth that kept me company, into all manner of vice and ungodliness.'

Home must have seemed bleak to him after the excitement and companionship of army life. His mother and sister were dead, his stepmother, in the years he was away, must have established her own way of life in the home, and he almost certainly felt a desperate need to get away. Yet he had to stick to the only work available to him with his father.

Was it on his travels from place to place that he met the kind orphan girl who had loved and admired her own father for his goodness and godliness? Did she take pity on the lively imaginative young man, who seemed so strong and who loved all sport yet who at heart seemed lonely—often dispirited? Was he, perhaps, drawn to her because she was clearly intelligent, for her father's books were very precious to her?

Whatever brought them together is not known, but probably in 1648 or 1649 they did marry, young and vulnerable and both lonely. There is no record of the girl's name, but she probably came from another village, or even from Bedford. If this is so, it explains why no marriage is recorded in the registers of Elstow Church, and it is likely that they were married before a Justice of the Peace, as was the custom during Commonwealth when Cromwell ruled the country.

One can imagine that the young girl had been very

desolate, for she had lost a loved father, and there was no mother to give her any gift for a wedding. Years later John Bunyan left us a poignant picture of the young people:

> Presently after this, I changed my condition into a married state, and my mercy was, to light upon a Wife whose Father was counted godly: this Woman and I, though we came together as poor as poor might be, (not having so much household-stuff as a Dish or Spoon betwixt us both), yet she had for her part, *The Plain Man's Path-way to Heaven*, and *The Practice of Piety*, which her Father had left her when he died.

From this it seems that no gift for the marriage was given from John Bunyan's home. But he and his wife must have scraped and struggled to make a home together. They lived in a plain small cottage at Elstow, on the west side of the road from Bedford. It has gone now, but an old print shows it as having on either side of the door a latticed window with a wooden shutter to cover it at night. In the thatched roof are two latticed dormer windows and at one end was a lean-to forge. The house was probably white-washed. In this place they made their own happiness, and John, who was always deft with his fingers, and able to fashion different articles in both wood and metal, would have made their first simple pieces of wooden furniture.

Something remarkable now occurred. The young man, so hostile to spiritual things, found in his wife the goodness he had secretly longed for. He had always admired what he took to be real goodness, but he became violently disillusioned and distressed when people so often proved false to the image he had of them. Now he began to discover the beginnings of what he was subconsciously looking for. After the day's work was over he and his young wife would sit and read together—not exciting tales of romance or adventure or war such as the travelling chapmen carried around, but the two books his wife had brought as her only dowry. The first, the little vellum-bound square book, *The Plain Man's Pathway to Heaven*, was by Arthur Dent, parish minister of Shoebury, in Essex. It was a dialogue between four people who have a long May day to pass. They go and sit under an oak tree where there is 'a goodly arbour and handsome seats', and here in the shade they talk about 'heavenly matters'. The book aimed to instruct, so that 'every man may clearly see, whether he shall be saved or damned'.

It described the signs of salvation, so that the reader could see if he found them in himself. They included, a delight in God's word, the Bible; 'Often and fervent praier'; 'Patient bearing of the crosse, with profit and comfort'; and 'Honest, just and conscientious dealing in all our actions among men'. In short, it laid out the Puritan ideals and beliefs. It went on to describe signs of a man's 'damnation', signs such as 'seldome and cold prayer', pride, 'whoredome', swearing, and lying, which, with a number of other 'signs' the writer described as 'plague-sores' on a man. It was particularly severe about swearing, and this must have struck Bunyan forcibly for, as he later recorded, he had 'from a childe…few Equals—both for cursing, swearing, lying and blaspheming the holy Name of God'.

Today the book would be considered horrific in its literal picturing of the death of an unsaved soul, as, beset with devils, it is carried away into eternal damnation. Yet Puritans also studied the other side of the picture most intensely: the joyful certainty of forgiveness for the 'saved' man or woman who turned from his sins in repentance, and claimed for his salvation the atoning death of Christ who was the only mediator between God and Man. This often gave the Puritans a gentle and serene happiness and assurance.

The other book *The Practice of Piety* written by Lewis Bayly, later Bishop of Bangor, was published in 1612. By 1673 it had been printed fifty times in England and had also been translated into a number of other languages. Although it was by a leader of the Established Church of England, it found favour with many Puritans. It was one answer to the conflicting beliefs and enmities described in the last chapter, for the writer said it was 'An endeavour to extract out of the chaos of endless controversies the old practice of true piety which flourished before these controversies were hatched.'

Today these books might seem very heavy and dull reading yet John Bunyan, rebel to piety, lover of gaiety, of dancing and all sport and merrymaking, was seriously affected as he sat reading with his wife. Something new and fresh was beginning to stir in his mind. 'In these two Books,' he said, 'I should sometimes read with her, wherein I also found some things that were somewhat pleasing to me.' What had he begun to glimpse? Only, perhaps, a fleeting hope of a new and better way of life for he wrote: 'All this while I met with no conviction.' However, it is clear that, on the human level, he had found in his wife the love and security he greatly needed. And all the time she was gently but surely trying to change the direction of his thoughts:

> She would be often telling me of what a godly man her Father was, how he would reprove and correct Vice, both in his house, and amongst his neighbours; what a strict and holy life he lived in his day, both in word and deed.

Something resulted that must have amazed his former village friends and companions. The books had made him wake up, he wrote later, to his 'sad and sinful state', and he began to be fascinated by religion. In this situation, he turned to what Elstow could offer him, not realizing, perhaps, that he had tentatively taken the first steps on a journey that was to last the rest of his life. He started to go to the parish church twice on Sunday, taking his place among the regular churchgoers of the time. The vicar, a certain Christopher Hall was certainly not a Puritan. He was devoted to the episcopalian traditions in the Church of England, to the rule of bishops and the set services and liturgy from the prayer book. Bunyan, who had an acute perception of beauty, as his writing was to show later, loved the church services, the ritual, the beautiful words and the singing. The vicar seemed to him almost a heavenly being. He wrote:

> I adored, and that with great devotion, even all things, (both the High-place, Priest, Clerk, Vestments, Service, and what else) belonging to the church; counting all things holy that were therein contained; and especially the Priest and Clerk most happy, and without doubt greatly blessed, because they were the Servants, as I then thought, of God, and were principal in the Holy Temple, to do his work therein.

His pent-up emotions, his longing for goodness and beauty, his warm, enthusiastic and fervent nature are never more vividly portrayed than here. He was prepared to give the priest great devotion, indeed any priest seemed to him a marvellous person, and with his highly imaginative nature, which was to enable him to write so fluently and colourfully in later life, he was now fascinated by those men who seemed so far above him, and worthy of his admiration. This feeling grew so strong that he wrote of it later:

> Had I but seen a Priest (though never so sordid and debauched in his life) I should find my spirit fall under him, reverence him, and knit unto him; Yea, I thought for the love I did bear unto them, (supposing they were the Ministers of God) I could have layn down at their feet, and have been trampled upon by them; their Name, their Garb, and Work, did so intoxicate and betwitch me.

When, in middle life, Bunyan, as a convinced Puritan, reflected on this time in his life, he saw it as a period of spiritual blindness. He wrote that he had been 'overrun with the spirit of superstition'. Always harsh in his judgements of himself, he failed to recognize the passionate longing side of his nature, the capacity for ardent devotion that needed to be expressed. He only saw that he had been unaware then of the evil of sin, and hardly even able to recognize the reality of Christ. At that time he knew nothing of the dark night of the soul he was about to experience, or of the pilgrimage on which, before long, he must set out—to 'the City of God'.

CHAPTER 5

The Father

In the year 1650, when John Bunyan was twenty-two, his wife gave birth to a girl. Although everything he wrote years later testifies to his gentleness and tenderness with all children, this child was to become particularly dear to him. When they carried her across the green to Elstow Church one July day, to be baptized and christened Mary, did they know or suspect that all was not well with her? He developed a passionate protective love for her, writing that she lay 'nearer his heart' than all else in the world. The reason was tragic. She was blind.

What effect this sorrow had on him cannot be fully known. Did he feel, as many religious people of the time did, perhaps especially the Puritans, that troubles and disasters were a judgement from the hand of God? At first nothing in his manner seemed wrong. He worked tirelessly and with immense energy to support his little family. He still took a vigorous and leading part in sports and dancing on the green. A contemporary anonymous biographer described him as 'tall of stature, strong boned, though not corpulant, somewhat of a Ruddy Face, with sparkling eyes...' and we can picture a young man of great vitality. But, almost imperceptibly, something in him was changing.

He had an increasingly uneasy conscience and, at times, fell into moods of depression and black despair. Then he would hurl himself into his sport with his friends, and push the troubles to the back of his mind.

Things came to a head one Sunday morning. In church that Sunday the Reverend Christopher Hall preached on the importance of keeping the Sabbath Day holy, and the sin of breaking it with sports or work. Unfortunately Sunday was probably the only time John Bunyan was free for sport, as he needed to work tirelessly during the week either in the forge or travelling from village to village. He was shattered by the sermon, and felt it was especially directed at him. He was seized with a dreadful feeling of guilt. He went home, he said, 'with a great burden upon my spirit'. His feelings swayed to and fro, but a good meal was waiting for him, and he recounts that before he had finished eating, the trouble began to pass from his mind. His spirits rose, and he felt sure the trouble had gone from him, and that he could go and 'sin' again, 'without controul'. Cheered by the food, he 'shook the sermon' out of his mind, and went over to the village green to play the popular game of tipcat. This game was played with the cudgel and the 'cat', rounders probably being the nearest thing to it today.

Suddenly, in the middle of the game, when he had just struck the 'cat' one blow from the hole, and was about to strike it again, he seemed to hear a voice from heaven which, he later wrote, struck into his soul. Like Paul on the Damascus road, he was thunderstruck. He looked up to the heavens, and there and then his thoughts produced a sort of vision or mental picture of 'the Lord Jesus looking down upon me', as he described it, 'very hotly displeased with me, and as if he did severely threaten me with some grievous punishment for these, and other my ungodly practices'.

The terrible thought flashed upon him that it was now too late for him ever to hope to go to heaven. He had gone too far. This appalled him, and he said he felt sure that 'Christ would not forgive me, nor pardon my transgres-

sions'. These vivid and terrifying thoughts show how far
he was from having any clear understanding at that time
about Christ's teaching on forgiveness and salvation. The
Puritans were apt to preach with fierce warnings of the
dangers of judgement for sinners, of hell and 'the wrath to
come'. Some painted fearful word pictures of the horror
of being eternally separated from Christ as a punishment
for deliberately choosing to reject him. They tended to
drive converts into the kingdom of heaven with the whip of
fear, rather than drawing them in with the teaching of
Christ's love for the sinner.

In the middle of the game he stood silent among his
companions, who must have been surprised at his behaviour. At last, he records, he thought that, since there
was now no hope for him, if he had to be damned for
ever, he might as well be damned for many sins as for few.
Probably something of his old rebelliousness surfaced and
he began to feel the strongest desire to take his fill of sin,
and 'to taste the sweetness of it'. 'Before God,' he wrote,
'these were really, strongly, and with all my heart, my
desires; the good Lord, whose mercy is unsearchable,
forgive me my transgressions.' But now all happiness had
gone. 'I returned desperately to my sport again,' he said,
but despair possessed his soul.

Reckless in his behaviour, but with secret misery, he
went on in this way for a month or more, until one day he
was standing outside a neighbour's shop window, cursing
and swearing and 'playing the Mad-man, after my wonted
manner'. The woman of the house, whom he describes as
'a very loose and ungodly wretch', heard him. She came
out, and rounded on him, saying that it made her tremble
to listen to him. She told him he was 'the ungodliest
fellow' for cursing and swearing that she had heard in her
whole life, and that he was capable of spoiling all the
young people in a whole town if he ever came near them.

Bunyan was suddenly full of shame. Hanging his head,
he fell silent, and at that moment felt totally inadequate.

His overriding wish was that he could be a child again so
that his father could take him in hand and, as he later
recorded, 'learn me to speak without this wicked way of
swearing'. It seemed hopeless now even to try to change.
But he was terrified of going to hell and somehow he did
make the effort. He was surprised and then thankful to
find he could leave off his swearing. Moreover, he found
he could speak better, 'and with more pleasantness', than
ever before. Yet something was still missing. He went on
with his sports and play, and though today this all seems
innocent enough, to him it meant restlessness in his soul,
and the feeling that all was not well.

Recording his spiritual journey years later in *Grace
Abounding to the Chief of Sinners,* he describes a small
event of some significance which took place at this time.
Perhaps in the course of his work, Bunyan met a 'poor
man', probably a Puritan from his description, 'who made
profession of Religion'. This man began to talk 'pleasantly
of the Scriptures' to Bunyan who enjoyed the conversation
and as a result started to read the Bible. He found he
much enjoyed the stories in the Old Testament, the history
of the Jewish people in their journeyings, battles and
search for God. But he could make little of Paul's letters
which were quite beyond his understanding.

The Ten Commandments he could well understand, and
he tried hard to keep them. Honest as always, he had to
confess that on the whole he thought he was doing well,
until now and then he broke one. Then he felt conscience-
stricken. Full of repentance he would promise God that
he would do better next time, and with this he felt he must
really please God very much, 'as well as any man in
England'.

The neighbours in Elstow began to marvel at the change
in Bunyan, and began to think of him as 'a new and
religious man', for he was now outwardly leading a moral
and upright life. They began to praise him and speak well
of him. 'Oh,' he wrote, with wry honesty, 'it pleased me

mighty well.' He added the comment: 'I was nothing but a poor painted Hypocrite.'

He was beginning to fight a great battle of conscience. He decided his pleasure and amusements must be given up. From today's standpoint it seems sad that he felt they were all sinful. But, though his understanding was partly clouded, he was seeking the one thing that mattered, the thing that meant more than anything in the world, the pearl of great price. He was setting out to find God and the promise of eternal life. Everything else had to go.

Bunyan had become a bellringer at Elstow Church. He rang one of the bells housed in the steeple-house, a tall stone building which stood beside, but separate from, the church. He loved bellringing, but, perhaps through the influence of the man who had interested him in the Bible, he began to think that 'such a practice was vain'. In his heart he greatly hankered after the ringing and only after forcing himself by a great effort was he able to give it up. Yet he so longed to do it that he used to go and watch the ringers, standing quite close to them. Then, fearful of judgement for sin, he began to imagine one of the bells might fall on him. His imagination ran riot. He pictured one of the bells swinging out, hitting the wall, ricochetting and hitting him with tremendous force and killing him. So he thought he had better stand in safety in the steeple-house doorway, where he could slip out safely behind the thick walls if a bell should fall. Now his mind began to be tortured by wild imaginings. He thought the whole steeple-house might perhaps collapse and fall on him and kill him. He dared no longer even stand at its door. His days with the bellringers were over.

The last struggle was to give up dancing. He was passionately fond of it, and it took a whole year to tear himself away from it; but when he had at last done so his conscience was for a time at peace. He felt again that he must surely please God as well as any man in England. But all the while he was, he said, 'ignorant of Jesus Christ'.

CHAPTER 6

What Shall I Do to Be Saved?

John Bunyan's new interest in religion gripped him. He was secretly much gratified by his neighbours' admiration of his outwardly changed life. Always fluent—a gift that was going to be of enormous value in the future—he now began to talk about religion to others, and, listening to himself, he was rather pleased at his ease of expression. 'I was a brisk talker,' he confesses. But this mood did not last long.

The four years following his marriage were to see him experience an agonizing spiritual conflict that was so deep that it almost affected his sanity. In *Grace Abounding to the Chief of Sinners* which he wrote in prison years later, he painted a dark and sombre picture of his mental distress, and was merciless in judging himself.

Having given up all sports and amusements, he had begun to see his life from the standpoint of the more rigid Puritans, but he had discovered none of the serenity and joy which coloured the hearts and minds of many of the gentler and more understanding of them. He began to be deeply anxious about the sins of his mind and soul, as he saw them, not about the more obvious sexual sins. In fact, he confessed very frankly later in life that he was rather shy of women, and always lived a moral life, totally faithful to his wife. To him, his wrongdoing was far worse. He

45

believed he had, up to that time, rejected God deliberately and knowingly. All he could do, he thought, was to work hard for the salvation of his soul.

His fear was the greater because he was influenced by some of the teaching of Calvin which coloured much Puritan thought. One of Calvin's beliefs was that God, knowing all things, must know who would eventually repent and become a believer and who would not. Bunyan had a simple and, some might say, superficial understanding of this doctrine of predestination, believing, as many did, that certain people were actually destined to be saved, while others were destined for eternal punishment. This fearful thought preyed on his mind, and became an intolerable burden. Was it his destiny to be shut out for ever from salvation because of his own misdoings? To this question he could find no answer.

An important step in his desperate search for salvation came one day when, in connection with his ordinary work, he went to Bedford. Walking through the streets he suddenly saw a little group of three or four poor women sitting on a doorstep in the sun talking together. Something about them rivetted his attention. He paused. They looked so happy, and he longed for happiness. They had something about them which was instantly recognizable to him, a sort of holiness which he had never met before. He drew nearer. 'They talked,' he said, 'as if joy did make them speak.' At first he could understand very little of what they were saying, for they spoke of a new birth, of how God had worked in their hearts, and how they knew they were sinners by nature, but how God had visited their souls with his love through the Lord Jesus. They spoke of the words and promises in the Bible which comforted and sustained them, and supported them against the temptations of the Devil. Bunyan looked and listened with longing. They were, he thought, like people who had found a new world. They were quite different from all their neighbours.

Bunyan's experience was not new. All through the centuries Christians who have opened hearts and minds wholly to God's Spirit have something beautiful and indefinable about them, however ordinary they may be in themselves. Those who have met Mother Teresa of Calcutta, for example, understand this. To see something of Christ in someone can be too much for some people. It is like seeing the sun with the naked eye; it scorches the soul and they turn away. For others there is a solemn and joyful recognition and in their hearts they cry out, 'At last! I have seen that which I have been searching for all my life!' So it was for Bunyan. But as yet he only desperately wanted what they had, he did not know how to get it. 'I felt my own heart began to shake,' he wrote, describing that day, for he found he knew nothing whatever about a new birth, nor about words of comfort and promise in the Bible.

He left Bedford, but the words of the women would not leave his mind. Again and again he made excuses to go back and join their little group to listen to all they had to say. He was like a starving man craving food, but it was food for the soul not the body for which he was desperately searching. Two things resulted from his visits to the women. First, he began to love the great biblical truths which they were beginning to teach him in their simple way—a simplicity that was the outcome of a profound and steady faith, rather than of anything superficial. Secondly, he began to meditate deeply on the words of the Scripture, poring over them, and weighing up what they actually taught him. Above all, he realized his ignorance and lack of knowledge: 'God knows, I knew but little,' he wrote.

This new interest filled his life. He gave up old friends who had no sympathy with the new direction of his life. To perhaps his best former friend he said, 'Why do you curse and swear thus? What will become of you if you die in this condition?' The old friend had a very quick and scornful answer to that: 'What would the Devil do for company if it were not for such as I am?' he said, and so they parted, and Bunyan was alone in his search for salvation.

But now he had a new companion, the Bible. It became inexpressibly precious to him, although at times certain texts were to terrify him, and give him a feeling of despair, for he could not find out how to get eternal life. He was, he said, never away from his Bible, and kept constantly 'crying out to God to know the truth, and the way to Heaven and Glory'. Bunyan had had no real teaching about the Bible except from the women. He read it simply as from the hand of God, given by inspiration through the ages to holy men of God. In fact, down the years since the time of Christ, and up to this day many have found a strong Christian faith simply through reading the Bible, particularly the New Testament, which has come alive for them.

When, years later, Bunyan pictured Christian in *The Pilgrim's Progress*, he described himself at this stage in his life, just beginning to take the first steps of a great journey which would lead him through many dark places, many dangers and times of testing, but kept going all the way by the vision of joy inexpressible at the end. So poor Christian, like Bunyan, sets out:

> Now I saw, upon a time, when he was walking in the fields, that he was (as he was wont) reading in his book, and greatly distressed in his mind; and as he read, he burst out as he had done before, crying, What shall I do to be saved?

CHAPTER 7

The Dark Night of the Soul

Bunyan's great desire after his first meeting with the Bedford women was to discover if he had faith or not. This seemed to him exceedingly important, because, he said, 'I saw for certain, if I had not, I was sure to perish for ever.' The terrifying thought that his soul must be in mortal danger, caused him endless distress. Eventually it brought him to the brink of madness, and many a weaker character might have been destroyed by such spiritual anguish. But Bunyan was young and strong, and he had an absolutely unbreakable determination to find an answer. His overactive mind, however, led him on some strange paths.

He decided one day to put himself to a real test to discover if he truly now had faith. Had not Christ said that if a man had enough faith he could actually move mountains? The words, of course, expressed a profound truth in pictorial or symbolic language. But Bunyan took all the words of the Bible completely literally, and he believed Jesus was referring to a real mountain. He decided he would try out his possible faith on something smaller. On the rough country roads around his home, the horses' hooves left deep prints, which filled up with water after rain. Gazing at these, he decided to say to the rain-puddles, 'Be dry', and to the dry places, 'Be you the puddles'. But as he looked it did seem difficult, and he felt he must pray for faith to perform his miracle. He went and knelt under a hedge to ask God for faith to do this thing. After he prayed earnestly his mind turned restlessly this way and that, and he knew that if the miracle did not take place, he would have to accept that he had no faith. This he could not face. He turned away and concluded despairingly that he would never be able to find true faith. At this he was so perplexed that he did not know what to do.

All through this time, which lasted well over two years, he was tormented and yet haunted by the peace and happiness of the Bedford women. The sense of being an outsider, of being one who could find no way to belong to the blessed people of God, preyed on his mind. In the end it caused him to have a sort of vision or dream.

He saw the little group of women sitting in bright sunlight on one side of a high mountain, happy in the warmth and the golden light. But he found himself on the other side of the mountain, where he shivered in bitterly cold weather with frost and snow about him. Above him were dark clouds, and a strong wall separated him from the women in the sun. He knew that somehow he must reach them. Again and again he examined the wall, but could find no way through, until at last he discovered a tiny gap like a little door in it. He frantically tried to climb through, but his frenzied efforts met with no success and he became utterly exhausted. He made another superhuman effort and squeezed his head through, and then his shoulders and at last the rest of his body. Overcome with joy, he went and sat down among the women, comforted by the light and heat of the sun.

Bunyan thought over this dream-vision, which became stronger than reality to him. It became clear to him that the mountain represented the church of the living God, and the sun was the shining or favour of God's face upon it. The wall was the word of God showing the separation between Christians and the world. The gap in the wall was

Jesus Christ, the Way, just as he had said. Now Bunyan longed above all to be one who sat in the sunshine. As he walked through the fields or worked at the forge, or sat by the fire in the evenings, he would pray, in the words of Psalm 9, 'O, Lord, consider my trouble.'

As he turned this way and that in search of assurance, he was more than ever tormented by the thought that probably he was not one of God's elect or chosen people destined for salvation. Perhaps the Day of Grace—the time when men can still freely choose whether or not they will turn to God—was over and past. His distress deepened. He records that he 'was in a flame to find the way to Heaven and Glory'. Now physical symptoms appeared. He began to feel very weak, unable to face the thought that unless God in mercy had chosen him, John Bunyan, to be one of his own, then none of his desire to find the truth would be any use. He felt faint when he tried to walk, and ready to sink down, with despair in his heart. Of course it is well understood in medical science today, that distress of mind causes weakness of the body, and doctors and counsellors can give medical and spiritual help. But Bunyan was alone, and no one could explain his situation to him. He blamed it entirely on what he saw as his past terrible sins.

Yet even at this time, various texts from the Bible would suddenly float into his mind, as if sent to him by God in answer to his desperate questionings. One sentence in particular brought him real comfort: 'Look at the generations of old, and see, did ever any trust in God and were confounded?' Then suddenly he felt as if a command from God was put into his mind: 'Begin at the beginning of Genesis and read to the end of the Revelations, and see if you can find that there was any that ever trusted in the Lord, and was confounded.' So back he went to his Bible, and began a tremendous search, but could not find the words at first, until at long last he found them in the Apocrypha which are included in some editions of the Bible, but are not considered inspired in the same way as the canonical books of Scripture. He was a little disappointed at this, wondering if they really were the words of God.

Once again a period of torment came on him and he wished with all his heart that he had turned to God when he was much younger. He became angry with himself at such great carelessness on his part, and wrote, 'To think that I should have no more wit but to trifle away my time till my Soul and Heaven were lost.' Texts continued to flood into his mind, and he alternated between hope and despair.

One day he remembered words from Luke's Gospel: 'Compell them to come in, that my house may be filled, and yet there is roome.' He wrote that these words, which seemed to offer him a place in heaven, were beautiful to him. He believed that Christ was speaking directly to him with these words.

Bunyan was still young, and he and his wife had three other children after blind Mary. Elizabeth, and later John and Thomas, were born during these years of struggle, and it must have been a full and probably noisy household with the children running in and out. He had to work extremely hard to support them all, and perhaps tiredness played its part in his anxiety and distress. Surrounded by people, he felt alone, shut off in a seemingly endless spiritual struggle.

The desire now gripped him to be called personally by Christ to follow him, as the first disciples had been called:

> Oh how I loved those words that spoke of a Christian calling! as when the Lord said to one Follow me; and to another, Come after me, and oh, thought I, that He would say so to me too! How gladly would I run after him. I cannot now express with what longings and breakings in my Soul, I cryed to Christ to call me.

He began to watch people closely when he knew they were converted and true followers of Christ. Such men and women seemed beautiful to him, for he saw in them an inner beauty independent of outward looks and he wrote that to him 'they shone'. Slowly the thought of a loving Christ rather than an angry God seems to have been entering his mind, although he never felt the call he greatly desired at that time. But he did experience a faint hope that one day he too might be converted to Christ, though just how he did not know.

At last, when these mental pressures must have built up intolerably inside him, he went to the only true friends he knew, the poor women of Bedford, who must have been full of compassion for this strong but sad young man. They clearly felt a deep interest in him. He was another soul to be saved for Christ's sake. They immediately wanted to help him and they did the best thing possible. They went to the pastor of their little meeting in Bedford and told him all about the young tinker. He at once talked with Bunyan, and invited him to his house to listen to discussions with other people about the dealings of God with the souls of men and women. So it was that John Bunyan met a truly remarkable man.

John Gifford was both vicar of the Parish Church of St John under Commonwealth ruling, and also minister of the small independent congregation to which the women belonged, and which met in the church. He had been a soldier, a major in King Charles I's army, who after Charles' defeat took part in the raising of troops to continue fighting against Parliament. For this he was condemned to death on the gallows with eleven other men. On the night before his execution his sister visited him in prison, and found all the guards were asleep. His companions had drunk themselves unconscious. Only he was awake she told him. Thereupon he walked quickly out of the prison, went as far as the nearby countryside and hid in a ditch in a field for three days until the search was over. Then friends brought him some clothes to wear as a disguise, and took him first to London, and then to Bedfordshire where he was hidden by Royalists. When at last the whole affair had been forgotten, he went to Bedford as a stranger, and began to practise as a physician, although, like many other so-called doctors, he was completely unqualified. During this time he led a wild and reckless life, drinking, gambling, constantly swearing and blaspheming. He was, also, a violent man, and at one point actually tried to murder a leading Puritan, Anthony Harrington.

One night he lost fifteen pounds at gambling, which was a very large sum in those days, and he had, as he later recounted, many angry and desperate thoughts against God. By chance he picked up a religious book and began to read it. It alarmed him and startled him, and the sudden realization dawned that he was a great sinner. This shocked him greatly. His whole life from that moment changed direction. He began to attend the meetings of the Puritans whom he had formerly hated and despised. Eventually, like Paul, he experienced a Damascus road type of conversion to Christ. It was so real, so vivid to him, that it held him and sustained him for the rest of his life.

At first the Puritans looked on him very suspiciously, just as the early Christians had looked at Saul of Tarsus. But at last he totally convinced them of his complete sincerity, and he began to preach. The sinner had become a saint, and was to become a greatly loved pastor, for in the end, eleven people formed themselves under his care as pastor, some being the poor women, and one that very Anthony Harrington whom he had once tried to murder. His life became so totally committed to Christ that he became known as 'holy Mr Gifford' to the people in Bedford.

The little fellowship of which he was pastor became the first members of the Bedford Meeting which was formed in 1650. This was one of the so-called 'gathered' churches which had separated from 'prelaticall superstition', or the ritual of the Church of England and the use of the Book of Common Prayer; it was the first such meeting in Bedford. The members met together on the basis of their faith in

Christ and holiness of life. Their worship was very simple: they read the Bible together, prayed together, and listened to sermons and discussions.

When years later Bunyan drew a beautiful picture of Evangelist who set Christian on his way and directed the first steps of his great journey, he based him on the character of Mr Gifford, who seemed to Bunyan so strong and faithful. Evangelist is pictured as a strong figure, Christian as a despairing one. We read:

> Then Evangelist gave him a parchment roll, and there was written within, Fly from the wrath to come. The man, therefore, read it, and looking upon Evangelist very carefully, said, Whither must I fly? . . . Evangelist said, Do you see yonder shining light? He said, I think I do. Then said Evangelist, Keep that light in your eye, and go up directly thereto, so shalt thou see the gate; at which, when thou Knockest, it shall be told thee, what thou shalt do.

So Christian leaves wife and children and home and runs with his fingers in his ears so that he will hear no one calling him back to stop him, and as he runs he cries, 'Life! life! eternal life!'

Strangely enough, now that Bunyan had friends anxious to help him, he found himself in the depths of depression and despair once again. He regarded his own case as so hopeless that he was strongly tempted to sin again. Temptations crowded in on him. He found he was caught in a snare like a bird: 'My heart would not be moved to mind that that was good, it began to be careless, both of my soul and Heaven; it would now continually hang back both to, and in every duty, and was as a clog on the leg of a Bird to hinder her from flying.' With such small homely pictures taken from his everyday life, Bunyan illustrates his sorrow and frustration. He felt like a 'loathsome' person in his own eyes and in God's. 'Now I grow worse and worse, now am I farther from conversion than ever I was before. . . . If now I should have burned at a stake, I could not believe that Christ had love for me.'

The people in Mr Gifford's congregation tried to comfort and help him. Perhaps they felt his condition was puzzling and obscure, for he seemed simply blind when presented with the way of salvation. Nowadays we would realize that his condition was the result of a deep depression, not easy to cure. 'My soul is dying, my soul is damning,' he lamented. He even began to envy the birds and animals around him who were not destined for hellfire as he felt sure he was. The Bedford Meeting people tried to comfort him with the great biblical promises, but to no avail. 'They might as well have told me to reach the Sun with my finger,' he said. Worse still, he found he had turned against God and the Bible.

The root cause of much of his distress was his dreadful fear of the eternal damnation of his soul. This terror held him in a remorseless grip. No sorrow seemed as bad as his. The mental conflict seemed unrelenting. Yet even at this time he did not stay away from the Meeting and his pastor and friends. Presently after months of this terrible state of mind, 'a time of comforting', as he described it, came to him.

He heard a sermon, not about judgement, but about love—the love of Christ for the soul of man. He heard the final words, 'Poor tempted Soul, when thou art assaulted and afflicted with temptation, and the hidings of God's face, yet think on these two words, *my love*, still.' It was the message he needed. It might have been spoken for him. A sudden warmth came into his poor tortured mind, and the words 'Thou art my Love' repeated themselves on and on in his thoughts, making, he said, 'a joyful sound in my soul'.

He was flooded with sudden happiness. He could hardly contain himself until he got home to tell his wife, who for so long must have been gravely worried about him. He wrote, 'I thought I could have spoken of his *love*, and of his mercy to me, even to the very Crows that sat upon the plow'd lands before me.' At that moment he was so happy that he wished he had pen and ink to record his feelings exactly, so that he would never forget them all his life.

Sadly, as in many depressive illnesses, although this marked the beginning of some improvement, he slipped back again a month later into the despairing doubts and questionings. He began to hear an insistent voice in his head. It was, he felt sure, Christ speaking to him, and so clearly that he turned round to see who it was behind him. The voice said, in Christ's words to Peter: 'Simon, Simon, behold Satan hath desired you.' Once more he felt at the heart of a great cosmic conflict between God and the Devil.

Now the storm in his mind began to reach its height. Darkness, he later wrote, seized upon him. To his horror he found terrible blasphemies against God, Christ and the Bible pouring from his mouth. He began to wonder if God and Christ were even real. Was the Bible nothing more than a fable? So terrible did he find his thoughts that he could not even record them later. Compulsive and neurotic ideas tore all peace from him, and this culminated in the appalling belief that he was possessed by the devil. Strange and wild behaviour followed. He sometimes felt like jumping head first into a muck-heap in order to silence his mouth from blaspheming. This terrible darkness of spirit lasted about a year. He began to believe that when praying he would see the devil in person. He imagined he felt him pluck at his clothes, stop him praying and fill him with wicked thoughts.

During these long months he alternated between this despair and brief flashes of trembling hope that his soul might not be damned for ever for his sins, which weighed so terribly upon him. He used to sit by the fire at home, thinking how wretched and hopeless he was. Hour by hour he pored over his Bible, searching for any words of comfort.

One day he recalled from Hebrews 2:14–15, 'Forasmuch then as the children are partakers of flesh and blood, he [Christ] also himself likewise took part of the same; that through death he might destroy him that had the power of death, that is, the devil, and deliver them who through fear of death were all their lifetime subject to bondage.' The effect of these words was dynamic. Joy once more came to him for it was a message exactly for him. He said, 'The glory of these words was then so weighty on me, that I was both once and twice ready to swoon as I sat, yet not with grief and trouble, but with solid joy and peace.'

He now went to Bedford Church to listen attentively to Mr Gifford, who greatly helped him and explained the great biblical doctrine of salvation. He listened with joy. His soul, he said, was now 'led from truth to truth'. As he read the New Testament he began to understand in depth the gospel of Jesus Christ. Now it was the most marvellous narrative to him. It came alive as he read. His imagination fed on it, aflame with joy, and he recorded that he actually seemed to see vivid pictures in his mind of the birth of Christ, his growing up, and his walk through the world. Then he watched how Christ gently gave himself to die upon the cross. In imagination he saw a beautiful picture of Christ leaping for joy as he left the tomb at the Resurrection.

It was at this time that he experienced growing longings to discover in some book the true experiences of another Christian, to see how faith had worked in someone else. It seemed providential to him that one day he came across a very old, very tattered book by Martin Luther. It was a translation of his *Commentary on Paul's Letter to the Galatians*. Fascinated, he began to read it. He was gripped. It described his own condition. He felt as if he himself could almost have written the book. It expressed his own feelings exactly, for Luther and Bunyan had both experienced the agony of a wounded conscience. Both had a torturing fear of eternal damnation. But Luther showed him the way of release through a clear understanding of

God's great mercy. Once more Bunyan's spirit soared. His love for Christ flamed up and filled him. He wanted to live close to him for ever. At that moment of happiness he was even ready to die.

But the long agony was not yet over. The battle had to go through its long final phase, and Bunyan experienced torment as never before which nearly destroyed him. The strange temptation came to him that he must 'sell' Christ. Shocked and numbed, he endured an endless repetition in his mind of the words 'Sell him', 'Sell him'. Now he was on the verge of complete breakdown; he believed his terrible experience was simply the result of his most sinful character. He could not eat or sleep. He found prayer impossible. He feared that the Devil would so wear him out that he would have no more strength left to fight, his will would be finally destroyed, and he would consent to 'sell Christ'. His fears brought strange physical symptoms. He was always pushing and thrusting with arms and elbows, as if to push something away. On and on the words rang in his brain, 'Sell him.' On and on he replied, 'I will not, I will not.' He was on the rack. If he began to eat he would have to leap up from meals to go and pray. Tortured in mind, his strength evaporated. He could hold out no longer.

One morning, lying in bed, the dreadful temptation came yet again: 'Sell him.' Utterly worn out, he gave silent assent with the words, 'Let him go if he will.' The terrifying realization of what he imagined he had done in betraying Christ finally broke him: 'Now was the battel won,' he wrote later, 'and down I fell, as a Bird that is shot from the top of a Tree, into great guilt and fearful despair.'

For two more terrible years he felt himself damned for ever. Occasionally he found a comforting text in the Bible that seemed to promise a little comfort. But relief was never more than temporary, for now he believed he was the worst sinner with whom God had ever had to deal, because, he thought, he had deliberately rejected Christ, and had sold him like Judas. He confessed that he became a burden and terror to himself, yet he was afraid to die. Now he suffered violent tremblings. Sometimes he felt his breast bone would fracture, so acute was the pain he experienced. Today he could have had medical and psychiatric treatment as well as the Church's Ministry of Healing to alleviate this distress. But in his day no one understood what was happening to him. His wife must have been exceedingly anxious, for he recounts that he could 'neither eat my food, stoop for a pin, drop a stick, or cast mine eye to look on this and that, but still the temptation would come'.

When years later he tells of the effect of Christian's behaviour on his friends and family in *The Pilgrim's Progress*, he is quite clearly describing his own situation:

> In this plight, therefore, he [Christian] went home, and restrained himself as long as he could, that his wife and children should not perceive his distress; but he could not be silent long because that his trouble increased...his relations were sore amazed...because they thought some phrensy distemper had got into his head; therefore, it drawing towards night, and they hoping that sleep might settle his brains, with all haste they got him to bed. But...instead of sleeping, he spent [the night] in sighs and tears. They also thought to drive away his distemper by harsh and surly carriages to him; sometimes they would deride, sometimes they would chide, and sometimes they would quite neglect him.

He went to work as usual, constantly read the Bible, desperately searching for comfort and consolation; above all he longed to be one of God's people. But he could not, indeed he found it impossible, to forgive himself. He became totally introverted, examining all his sins, real and imaginary, and comparing them with those of people in the Bible, including Judas. As ever his gift of words did not leave him, and he was later to describe these days as a time when he felt his 'soul, like a broken vessel, driven, as with the winds, and tossed sometimes headlong into dispair'.

He felt that all the world frowned on him. One day he sat on a seat in the town, and fell into deep thought about his fearful state, when suddenly he felt the sun grudge him its light, and the very buildings in the street turned against him, pressing in upon him to banish him or push him out of the world. Rational thought had completely left him.

In *Grace Abounding* he recorded one very curious experience from these days. He spoke cautiously of it, and could not explain it, yet it was a wonderfully consoling experience. He was walking backwards and forwards in a shop—his restless state is evident in every word—when 'Suddenly there was as if there had rushed in at the window, the noise of Wind upon me, but very pleasant, and as if I had heard a voice speaking, Didst ever refuse to be justified by the Blood of Christ?' He acknowledged that he had not refused, and suddenly light dawned in his mind, peace flooded into his heart, and he felt a great quiet within himself, because, he said, 'all those tumultuous thoughts that before did use, like masterless hell-hounds, to roar, bellow, and make a hideous noise within me ceased'. In that moment he felt that Christ had not cast him off for ever. It was an experience he could never explain afterwards.

Another comfort came with the words, 'My grace is sufficient for thee', which arrested him forcibly as he read the Bible. A great thankfulness flooded through him, and he had yet another vision or mental picture: 'It was as though I had seen the Lord Jesus look down from Heaven through the Tiles upon me, and direct these words unto me.' He felt as if his heart would break with joy, and for several weeks he had a sense of peace.

The outwardly small and insignificant events marking these terrible years of his life are described by Bunyan in colourful and dramatic terms, and seem to be like milestones in his mind, reminding him of the different stages of his spiritual journey.

Ultimately the great storm in his mind slowly subsided. He had asked the people of Bedford Meeting to pray for him, and they with Mr Gifford had supported him through the long months and years. He gained in understanding, and hope began to return. One day as he was once more walking in the fields, he suddenly saw in the eyes of his imagination Jesus Christ at God's right hand, and realized that his salvation came from Christ alone. 'Thy righteousness is in heaven' were the words which, he said, *sparkled* in his mind. No longer need he rely on his own efforts. *Christ had done it all for him*. At long last understanding had come and he found forgiveness and salvation and with it the certain hope of eternal life. Now, he said, 'Did my chains fall off my legs indeed, I was loosed from my affliction and irons, my temptations also fled away. Now Christ was all.' He was joined for ever to Christ in mystical union, and the dark night of his soul was past. The morning had come.

Nowhere is this time in his life more beautifully and movingly described than in *The Pilgrim's Progress*, when Christian comes to the foot of the cross, below which is a tomb. Here his heavy burden falls off his back into the tomb for ever. Christian's joy can hardly be expressed in words, but Bunyan gives an unforgettable picture of himself, the forgiven sinner:

> Then was Christian glad and lightsome, and said with a merry heart, He hath given me rest by His sorrow, and life by His death. Then he stood awhile to look, and wonder; for it was very surprising to him that the sight of the cross should thus ease him of his burden. He looked therefore, and looked again, even till the springs that were in his head sent the waters down his cheeks. Now as he stood looking and weeping, behold, three Shining Ones came to him, and saluted him with Peace be to Thee. So the first said to him, Thy sins be forgiven thee; the second stripped him of his rags, and clothed him with change of raiment; the third also set a mark in his forehead; and gave him a roll with a seal upon it, which he bid him look on as he ran, and that he should give in at the celestial gate: so they went their way. Then Christian gave three leaps for joy, and went on singing.

CHAPTER 8

The Preacher

John Bunyan joined the Bedford Meeting in 1653. He had
met with sympathy and loving care during his illness and
had been welcomed at Mr Gifford's house, where the
minister had talked with him and counselled him, and
Bunyan described how this had been 'much for my stability'. Probably at this same time, as a contemporary
writer later described, he stepped down into the water of
'Bedford river' in some quiet spot in the fields, to be
baptized by Mr Gifford.

In the same year John Gifford was offered a vacancy in
St John's Church, where he became the Rector. His little
independent congregation, who had met with him for
years, moved with him, and here Bunyan joined them.

For the next two years John Gifford was a true friend,
helper, teacher and guide to Bunyan. Probably for this
reason, and because he wanted to be near the church,
Bunyan moved his family into the town of Bedford in
1655, where they lived in St Cuthbert Street in the heart of
the town. He now joined in the fellowship of the church
fully, and found that the Lord's Supper or Holy Communion was a most precious feast to him. His struggles were
not quite over, however. To his horror, he experienced
yet another period of darkness when he found thoughts of
blasphemy coming into his head towards the Sacrament

and those who took it. Bewildered, he could only conclude that he had not approached the Sacrament with enough reverence. He prayed earnestly to be delivered from such thoughts, and presently the temptations passed, and he was able to take the bread and the wine in peace.

A new sorrow struck him in the same year that he went to live in Bedford. In the September of 1655 John Gifford became fatally ill and died while still in the prime of life. As he lay dying, he wrote a letter which, he said, he wanted to be read to his congregation on his death, and regularly thereafter. 'I beseech you, brethren beloved, let these words (wrote in my love to you and care over you, when our heavenly Father was removing me to the Kingdom of his dear Son) to be read in your church gatherings together.' He urged them to walk together in all love 'one to another' as Christ Jesus had loved them. As well as spiritual encouragement, he urged them to 'let no respect of person be in your comings together. When you are met as a Church there's neither rich nor poor, bond nor free, in Christ Jesus. 'Tis not a good practice to be offering places or seats when those who are rich come in.' The letter ended, 'Stand fast; the Lord is at hand.'

John Gifford was buried in the churchyard; and to this day there is a Bedford Meeting house, apart from the church, in a large and quite imposing building in the town, where his memory is still alive.

Bedford was quite a small town when Bunyan moved there with his wife and two little girls—Elizabeth, his second daughter, having been born the year before in Elstow, during the time of his terrible mental conflict. It was a town of between one and two thousand inhabitants. No 'foreigner' or person from a different town was admitted to the merchant guilds and no townsman was allowed to let his house to a 'foreigner', without the consent of the mayor. In fact outsiders were not welcome. The streets of the town were badly paved, and entrance into it at night ceased when all traffic over the bridge was stopped bet-

ween ten o'clock at night and five o'clock in the morning.
Perhaps there was a strong feeling of close community in
the town so that people living close to each other in the
narrow streets, knew each other well. In winter the town
was dark, but in the High Street lights were ordered to be
set up in winter outside the shops and business premises
and these were to be lit on opposite sides of the street on
alternate nights. A light was to consist of 'a candlelight of
the bignesse at least of sixteen in the pound'.

Bunyan's first years in Bedford proved to be a time of
both happiness and sorrow. His health began to trouble
him again for a time, and he thought he had consumption,
but probably it was simply the result of overstrain and
overwork, for he recovered. His sons, John and Thomas,
were born during these first years in Bedford. His home
was full of little children.

A new minister was appointed to the church, John
Burton, who won the people's love. His appointment was
recorded in the Registers of Ecclesiastical Appointments
in the Commonwealth which stated that John Burton 'is
by His Highness, Oliver, Lord Protector of England and
etc., under his seal manuall, nominated thereto'. It soon
appeared that he was far from strong and the Bedford
Meeting Church Book from 1656 on, when it began to be
kept, records the anxieties of his congregation about his
health.

It was in 1656 that John Bunyan first 'discovered' his
gift with words. It was to open an entirely new life to
him, and ultimately to bring him into great danger. He
was invited to 'speak a Word of Exhortation' at one of
the church meetings. Almost with fascination he described how 'Some of the most able among the saints
with us, I say the most able for Judgement, and holiness
of Life, did perceive that God had counted me worthy
to understand something of his Will in his holy and
blessed Word, and had given me utterance in some
measure to express, what I saw, to others for edifi-

cation.' When he was asked to speak in public, he wrote that it 'did much dash and abash my spirit'. He had a great sense of his own inferiority as always, yet this was coupled with an intense vitality which spurred him on to speak. Rather shyly he records that 'with much weakness and infirmity' he discovered his gift, and the people were moved and comforted and gave thanks to God for the grace given to him. From then on, the Church Book comments that from that time he began to preach regularly.

Even now he was not entirely immune from mental conflict. On one occasion he felt as if his body was broken, and as if his hands and feet were bound with chains. Suddenly the words 'I must go to Jesus' flashed into his mind. He turned to his wife—this is one of the rare occasions where she comes into his story—and said: 'Wife, is there ever such a scripture *I must go to Jesus*? She said she could not tell.' Suddenly, as he lay in bed lost in thought, he remembered words in the letter to the Hebrews, 'Ye are come . . . to Jesus the Mediator of the New Testament. . . . .' His spirit was at peace again, and he felt he could hardly lie still in his bed for the feeling of joy, peace and triumph through Christ.

On the whole, his mental struggles did not trouble him in their serious form much longer, and he was thankful. 'Blessed be God for having mercy on me,' he wrote as he finished his remarkable spiritual autobiography, *Grace Abounding to the Chief of Sinners*.

The Meeting now confirmed their confidence in Bunyan's gift by appointing him to public preaching. He himself had only undertaken the work after a time of solemn prayer and fasting. The congregation received him with joy and assured him that his words to them were edifying. Bunyan had an amazingly active mind, overactive often, a sense of drama, a remarkable talent in using words powerfully and often poetically, and a very vivid imagination. In a sense he was an artist, who could conjure up brilliant pictures in a few words. Yet at the same time he used the language of ordinary people, of the poor and the uneducated. He used the imagery of the countryside, field and farm, animals and birds, the home and the forge, all familiar to his listeners. He had an earthiness that linked his poetical thoughts to reality, and he spoke with tremendous power. The boy and young man who had so often 'played the madman', had now something of the talent of an actor. He was totally involved in the great divine drama, and he could move his audience to tears. Above all, his preaching reflected the thought and teaching of the Bible, which had literally become part of the pattern of his thinking and faith. His words echoed with the great biblical themes, with the poetry of the Psalms, the stern warnings of the prophets, the call to repentance of Paul, and, more and more strongly as time went by, the love of Christ.

The brethren in the Meeting took him around the countryside to preach in the villages. He felt humbled when he saw the effect his words had, yet was also astonished and delighted that God had allowed him, John Bunyan, the poor tinker, to speak as his witness. He was a sinner saved by grace, who preached to other sinners from his own dark experience. 'I have been as one sent to them from the dead,' he said. For two years he stressed the need for sinners to leave their sins and repent. As greater comfort grew in his own heart, he preached more of the grace and love of Christ, and then of the soul's union with Christ. Sometimes he tried to describe what his preaching meant to him and what he hoped to achieve. He said, 'I had not preached long before some began to be touched by the Word, and to be greatly afflicted in their minds at the apprehension of their sin and of their need for Jesus Christ.'

Above all, he had one great aim: 'In my preaching I have really been in pain, I have, as it were, travailed to

He began to preach in the villages, saying, 'I have been as one sent to them from the dead (page 67).

bring forth children to God.' The results were astonishing: 'they came by hundreds, and that from all parts' to listen to him.

His preaching was not without cost. Sometimes he felt such a weakness and faintness overtake him that his legs would hardly carry him into the pulpit. He had to face fierce opposition from the 'Doctors and Priests of the Countrey'. They despised the 'wandering preaching tinker' who was still only in his early thirties. The writer of a little sketch of Bunyan's life published in 1700 recounts that a Cambridge scholar said to him that he had heard that Bunyan was going to preach in a certain village church. Rather the worse for drink, the scholar said he was resolved 'to hear the tinker prate'. So he went into the church to laugh, but stayed to listen, and as a result was himself converted and became a preacher. Another well-known Cambridge man, Henry Denne, wrote to a Cambridge Professor, opposing his attacks on Bunyan, and said, 'You seem to be angry with the tinker because he strives to mend souls as well as kettles and pans.'

The times in which Bunyan began to write and preach were troubled and unsettled. At midnight on January 8th 1657, a determined attempt was made to set fire to Whitehall Palace and kill Oliver Cromwell. It failed. A day of thanksgiving for his deliverance was set aside, and some in Parliament thought he should be made king with a succession of male heirs. William Dell, a strong and influential man, the Rector of Yeldon, episcopally ordained but with Puritan sympathies, was one of those who strongly opposed this, believing it would lay the foundation for 'a new, most bloody and desolating war'. Cromwell, in fact, held the same view and in the same year refused the kingship, saying: 'I cannot undertake this Government with the title of King; and that is mine Answer to this great and mighty business.' But there was considerable unrest in the country.

Bunyan's own life was before long shattered by the death of his wife, leaving four young children in the house. To whom did he turn in this despairing situation, and in the great loneliness which must have gripped him? There is no record, no reference in his books to answer this, although the members of Bedford Meeting undoubtedly rallied around him to help. Was it possible that a girl of seventeen or eighteen had been coming in to help with the children during his wife's illness? We do not know. But it is a possible conjecture that there was such a girl to whom he turned for help with the children. All we know is that in the following year, 1659, Bunyan, now thirty-one, married Elizabeth, a girl of seventeen or eighteen. She was to become a very brave and loyal wife to him, caring for his little children faithfully, and somehow coping with the terrible times that followed.

It seems possible that she had been in the house before his wife's death, because at some unspecified time the terrible and most cruel rumour was put about, as he recounted, that 'I had my Misses, my Whores, my Bastards, yea, two wives at once.'[1] Bunyan's new fame had undoubtedly caused jealousy, but this went far beyond that, and he felt it was the Devil trying to overthrow his ministry. Other rumours were spread abroad—that he was a witch, a Jesuit, and a highwayman—all so totally ridiculous that they hardly needed to be answered. But he did reply, and that in the frankest and strongest terms to the accusations of immorality. In *Grace Abounding to the Chief of Sinners*, he wrote:

> My Foes have mist their mark in this their shooting at me. I am not the man, I wish that they themselves be guiltless, if all the Fornicators and Adulterers in England were hang'd

---

[1] This reference may, however, allude to the events described in chapter 13.

by the Neck till they be dead, John Bunyan, the object of their Envie, would be still alive and well.

He goes on to say that he has been shy of women since the time of his first conversion: 'It is a rare thing to see me carry it pleasant towards a Woman.... Their company alone I cannot away with.'

He affirms that the only woman closely known to him is his wife. Moreover, he asserts, he has been kept from immorality not because of goodness in himself but, 'God has been merciful to me, and has kept me, to whom I pray that he will keep me still, not only from this, but from every evil way and work, and preserve me to his Heavenly Kingdom.'

He had faced these slanders robustly and calmly. The terrible trial which next came to him was, he believed, the next assault of the devil to keep him from his preaching and from his service for Christ. If so, he, John Bunyan, was ready to stand against the fiery darts of the Evil One, come what might, and nothing would silence him. He was ready to fight in the fiercest battle of all for his Lord.

CHAPTER 9

The Arrest

The Church Book recording the activities of the Bedford Meeting indicate that by 1659 Bunyan was taking a more and more prominent part. He was constantly being used to go out on pastoral visits, encouraging the depressed, visiting the sick, or remonstrating with any who seemed to be acting wrongly. The work allocated to the deacons and leading members gives a vivid picture of the concern of the little group for each other's spiritual welfare. We read in one entry for February 27th 1659, for example:

> Our bro: Bunyan hath spoken with bro: Childe to come and render a reason of his withdrawing to some of the brethren and he refuseth to do it unless he may come before the whole congregation; we are agreed he have notice given him to come to the next Church meeting.

In all Bunyan's pastoral work it was his chief joy to go to 'the darkest places of the country', as he called them, so that he might preach to the poor, the ignorant and the uneducated, who, like him, had neither privilege nor wealth. Through this, and his preaching, he was becoming a very well-known figure, young and vigorous as he was, and ready to go long distances to preach.

How he fitted all this into his busy daily work as a

brazier can only be imagined, but he had to do so for he had to support his very young wife and the four little children at home. In fact he was fiercely independent, and had the pride of one who owed no man anything.

In one of his first small books, the writing of which was in itself an astonishing feat, he described himself as working constantly with his hands, for he said:

> Though I be poor and of no repute in the world, as to outward things, yet this grace have I learned, by the example of the Apostle [Paul] to preach the truth; and also to work with my hands, both for mine own living, and for those that are with me when I have opportunity.

As the member of a small separatist or Independent church, he believed that true Christians must be separated from the world and all its wrongdoing, and must not take part in any activity which would hinder or spoil their 'walk with Christ', as they called their Christian life. This meant that he did not rely on people to tell him what to do. He looked to God alone for guidance, as he prayed and as he read the Bible which was his charter for life.

Nevertheless he was bound to accept the judgement of the Bedford Meeting and on one occasion the entry indicated a mild reprimand. It read: 'Bro. Bunyan and bro. Childe having neglected to speak with Sister Chamberlaine and bro. Skelton; were again reminded of it and required to take care of it against the next meeting.'

Soon, however, the little internal affairs of the Meeting were to pale into insignificance before the storm that was threatening the country. Cromwell had died in 1658, and his son Richard had succeeded him as Protector, but he was totally unfitted for this position. There was great restlessness and discontent, and much talk about the Restoration of the Monarchy. The Independent churches and all those with Puritan sympathies, knew it would be a most anxious and dangerous time for them if this occurred.

history

Dislike of the strict Commonwealth rule had been strong
and bitter among all Royalists, and by the many Anglican
clergy and bishops who had been turned out of their
livings and dioceses under the Commonwealth rule. The
clergy who remained within the Established Church under
Cromwell were those who, with Puritan sympathies, followed Calvin's teaching, and believed that the church
should be governed by elders or 'presbyters', not by bishops and priests. For this reason they were called 'Presbyterians'. Under Cromwell the State Church admitted
clergy of three main Puritan Sects—Presbyterians, Inde-
pendents and Baptists—and there was religious tolerance,
except to Roman Catholics, and to high church clergy. So
those who had Royalist sympathies and the bishops and
ejected clergy were desperate to see Charles II return.

On the last day of November 1659, the members of
Bedford Meeting solemnly gathered together, as is recorded in their Book, 'in solemn seeking God for the nation'.
Their other overriding anxiety was for the failing health of
their now much loved minister John Burton. Again, some
months later in April 1660, a day was appointed 'to be
seeking God with reference to the affairs of the nation and
the weakness of our bro. Burton'.

During these turbulent and anxious years, Bunyan,
the fighter for the Lord in his preaching, discovered he
had another gift. He could express himself to a wider
audience by writing. His first book was a little volume
called *Some Gospel Truths Opened*. He was only twenty-
eight when it was published, and it was a remarkable
feat for a man whose learning had come entirely through
constant reading and study of the Bible, and earnest
listening to the teaching of Mr Gifford and, following
him, John Burton. And his minister, John Burton, commended him in the preface, saying, 'This man is not
chosen out of an earthly but out of a heavenly university...the Church of Christ.'

1656

'Thrown off at heat', as the book has been described,

Quaker Belief

it was an attack on certain beliefs of the Quakers, then a
growing Independent Sect, whose members stressed
the presence of Jesus in our minds and hearts rather
than Jesus as a real person who lived and died for us.
They spoke of an inner light in every man, which was
heretical to Bunyan and the Puritans as well as to the
Established Church. It was an error, Bunyan believed,
that must be attacked so that other weaker Christians
should not be led away from the truth, and his book is a
remarkable defence of the historic truth of the person of
Jesus Christ.

He was quickly opposed by a young Quaker who
wrote a book defending Quaker beliefs. Bunyan, ever
the fighter, once more launched into battle. His second
book was published in 1657. It was called *A Vindication
of Gospel Truths Opened*. The battle was now fierce;
Bunyan attacked the Quaker, saying he was 'a proved
enemy to the truth', a man who was 'censorious and
(who) utters many words without knowledge'.

1657 ✓

His third book was published in 1658, a few days
before Cromwell died, and had the grim title of *A Few
Sighs from Hell*. It was a sort of sermon or commentary
on the story told by Jesus of the rich man, Dives, who
utterly ignored the starving beggar, Lazarus, outside
his gate. Today we should find it very heavy and full of
dreadful warnings, but it is interesting for two reasons.
First, it proved a very successful book, going into nine
editions in Bunyan's lifetime. Religion was a popular
subject, and in an age when death carried people off
with terrible rapidity, people were anxious to feel at
peace with God. Second, it is particularly interesting in
that it shows how concerned Bunyan was about the
great gulf between rich and poor in his day. He felt
'sent' to the poor, and here were words of comfort
indeed from Christ himself, whose care for the poor
and rejected and underprivileged gave Bunyan deep
comfort. They compensated for the scorn he experi-

1658 ✓

enced from those who mocked at a tinker having the effrontery to preach and to write. In the book he speaks of 'those rich ungodly landlords that so keep under their poor tenants that they dare not go out to hear the Word for fear that their rent should be raised, or they turned out of their homes'. This is, surely, a little piece of social history referring to the Royalist landlords of Puritan tenants. He describes the arrogant scorn of the rich man who will not help the sick beggar: 'What, shall I dishonour my fair sumptuous and gay house with such a scabbed creephedge as he?' But it was Lazarus who at his death was carried up to heaven, and the rich man who went to hell.

Bunyan by now had discovered that he was as fluent a writer as a preacher, and it must have been a great encouragement. His fourth book, published in 1659, was *The Doctrine of Law and Grace Unfolded*. It appeared at the time when Bedford Meeting was praying for the state of the nation, and the Puritans in England could only anticipate the future with deep apprehension. Yet the book is a strong statement of a buoyant faith. He writes, 'I saw through grace that it was the blood shed on Mount Calvary that did save and redeem sinners', and for all his life that was to be the central pivot of his faith.

On Christmas Day, 1659, a significant event occurred which must have brought Bunyan great encouragement. The same Rector of Yelden, William Dell, who had opposed the idea of Cromwell being made king, invited him to preach from his pulpit. Dell was an outstanding and forceful man, a Fellow of Emmanuel College, Cambridge, who had been Chaplain to the army under General Fairfax. Coming into contact with John Bunyan, he had recognized his sterling qualities, his boldness and courage in preaching, and his ability to move people's hearts.

In May 1660 King Charles II landed at Dover among

scenes of wild enthusiasm. There were bonfires, peals of bells, public feasts and merrymaking, endless proclamations and general festivity. At first it was as if everyone relaxed; the Puritan influence of Cromwell's government had been too strict. Moreover it seemed as if there would be religious freedom. Before consenting to come to England, and assume the crown Charles had issued a declaration, afterwards called the Declaration of Breda. In it he had promised liberty to tender consciences, and the assurance that no one should be disquieted for differences of opinion in religion, so long as such differences did not endanger the peace and safety of the realm. But these proved to be empty promises.

1660

Early in October 1660, the county magistrates in Bedford issued an order for the public reading in all churches of the Liturgy of the Church of England according to the Book of Common Prayer. At first, Bunyan probably did not realize that this affected him. His view of the Prayer Book liturgy was that of most Puritans. He regarded it as a relic of popery which he urged his people to 'touch not' if they would be true to the faith of Jesus Christ. One of his objections was that he regarded the set prayers as 'men's inventions'. How could he possibly pray to God sincerely and spontaneously from his heart if he simply used other men's words? Moreover it was the book used by those who bitterly opposed the Puritans. He was totally determined to be obedient in all spiritual matters to God alone, and to his conscience. At this time he had become very well known among the Independent Groups and elsewhere, and in the eyes of the Royalists he was a marked man.

When, with the return of the king, the tide turned against the Puritans, it turned violently. This was the time of revenge for all the Royalists who had suffered under the Commonwealth. Now the ejected incumbents and bishops who were still alive were sent back to their dioceses and parsonages and most of the Puritan clergy were turned out. It was about this time that the Bedford Meeting was turned out of the parish church. They were now without church or minister, for John Burton had died a very short time before. But much worse was to come.

On November 12th 1660, Bunyan went to hold a religious meeting in the little hamlet of Lower Samsell, about thirteen miles from Bedford. The service was to be held in a farmhouse standing in a field thickly surrounded by elm trees on three sides. Like many large old houses in the neighbourhood it was defended by a moat, whose drawbridge could be lifted at night. In the same field there was an old hawthorn tree under which Bunyan used to stand and preach. Then and for many years after it was known as 'Bunyan's Thorn'. Bunyan had promised to be with his friends at the appointed time, 'if', as he said, 'the Lord permits.' A promise never had to be broken in Bunyan's thinking, and so he travelled on horseback, probably, or even on foot, and arrived to find some of his friends already gathered there. But instead of the happy welcome he usually experienced, he found anxious whisperings and consultations. His friends told him that Mr Francis Wingate, a magistrate who lived nearby, had issued a warrant against him, and that if he persisted in preaching he would be arrested. They whispered to him that there was a watch around the house, which Bunyan sturdily described as ridiculous. It was as if, he said, 'We did intend to do some fearfull business to the destruction of the country.'

The farmer in whose house the meeting was to be held was clearly extremely nervous and questioned the wisdom of proceeding. Bunyan, fearless and very determined, felt this as undoubtedly an attack by Satan to prevent the word of God being preached, and refused to consider giving in. 'As for my friend,' he wrote later,

'I think he was more afraid for me than himself.' Bunyan was ready to go into battle for his Lord. The courage he showed, and his steadiness are seen in his next words, which have a heroic quality in them. 'No,' he said to his friend who was urging him to make his escape quickly, 'by no means, I will not stir, neither will I have the meeting dismissed for this. Come, be of good cheer, let us not be daunted. Our cause is good; we need not be ashamed of it; to preach God's word is so good a work that we shall be well rewarded even if suffer for it.'

Bunyan then left his friends, who were all clearly most anxious, and walked out of the house into the yard to consider the situation alone, and to pray and meditate on the right course of action. He knew that if he did leave and 'run' as he put it, it would be thought of very badly in the country where in his preaching he had made it his business to encourage others. People would think he was not so strong in deed as in word, and that would be a sign of weakness. If he ran away when there was a warrant out for him, his friends might also be afraid to stand fast when their time of testing came. Perhaps, he thought, God had chosen him, the poor tinker, to be the first to be opposed for his faith. What a privilege! Again, if he now left his friends, it would be a discouragement to the whole church, which in any case was in great difficulties, and he would surely be regarded as a coward, and a 'blasphemer of the gospel'. He was strong and ready to be a faithful soldier of Jesus Christ and to face his enemies. But the heartache that came to him as he thought of his very young wife, caring for his four little children all under nine years old, his 'sweet babes' as he called them, can only dimly be imagined. But the die was cast. Come what might he would not falter. He turned and went back into the house.

Friends had now gathered from the villages around, and were clearly in a state of great apprehension. Bun-

Just as Bunyan was starting to speak, the door burst open (page 81).

yan calmly began the meeting with prayer, and how
heartfelt it must have been on that day. Everyone then
opened their Bibles, but just as Bunyan was starting to
speak, the door burst open. The constable and Mr Wingate's man burst in, ordered Bunyan to stop preaching
and to go with them. Bunyan refused to go until he had
spoken some words of encouragement to his people.
Quietly and earnestly he told them that they saw how
they were prevented from having the opportunity to
speak and to hear the word of God. Clearly they were
likely to suffer for it. But it was a mercy, a privilege, to
suffer for so good a cause. They might, he said, have
been arrested as thieves or murderers, but he said,
'Blessed be God, it is not so, but we suffer as Christians
for well doing.'

At this, the constable grew angry and impatient and
wanted to take Bunyan away without delay. So they left
the house to go to Mr Wingate the Justice. It then
appeared that Mr Wingate was away that day. A friend
of Bunyan's who had probably followed in great anxiety, stepped forward offering to let Bunyan stay the
night with him, and guaranteeing to bring him to the
constable the next morning. This was allowed.

The next day Bunyan and his friend returned to the
constable, and all three walked through the fields
to Harlington House, the large and ancient house of
Mr Wingate, a staunch Royalist, whose father had died
early in the Civil War, when he himself had been taken
by his mother to Oxford for safety. There was even
a priest-hole under the roof where Royalists were
believed to have been secretly sheltered. Wingate was
bitterly opposed to the Puritans and to all who had
supported Cromwell.

Wingate, although a magistrate, was still only in his
thirties. He faced Bunyan, then only thirty-two himself,
across the table in the great hall of the house. First he
asked the constable what he found the people at Lower

Samsell doing when he made the arrest. On hearing that there were only a few people gathered there to hear Bunyan preach, and there was no sign of anything else, he seemed at first at a loss. Then he asked Bunyan what he was doing there, and why it was not enough for him to follow his lawful business of brazier instead of breaking the law by preaching. In fact, in claiming that Bunyan had broken the law, he had to fall back on an old statute from Queen Elizabeth's reign, because Charles II's Declaration of Breda promising liberty to those of 'tender conscience' still stood at that time.

Bunyan answered Wingate by saying that his intention of going to Lower Samsell, and to other places, was to instruct and counsel people to forsake their sins and 'to close with Christ', meaning to accept Christ's offer of salvation. He said that he could work as a brazier and preach also.

Wingate, hearing this, lost his temper, and said that he would 'break the neck of these meetings'.

Bunyan quietly answered, 'It may be so.'

Wingate insisted that Bunyan must find sureties for his good behaviour or else go to prison. Sureties were at once found, but Bunyan would not let his friends stand for him if it meant promising to give up preaching, for, he declared he would 'not leave speaking the word of God'. Wingate told him that in that case he must be sent to prison to be tried at the next Quarter Sessions, and at once left the room to make out the committal document or 'mittimus', as it was called.

While this was being prepared, Bunyan waited, and presently Wingate's father-in-law, Dr Lindall, the Vicar of Harlington, came into the room. Dr Lindall began to taunt and revile Bunyan, who later described him as 'that old enemy of the truth'. Dr Lindall very scornfully asked him what right he had to preach. Bunyan replied in the words of Peter: 'Let every man as he hath received the gift, minister the same one to another.'

'To whom is that spoken?' asked Lindall.

'Why,' answered Bunyan, 'to every man that hath received a gift from God.'

Lindall taunted him again by reminding him of Alexander the Coppersmith in the Book of the Acts who greatly opposed the Apostles. He was 'aiming 'tis like at me, because I was a tinker,' Bunyan wrote later. But he had a quick reply for Lindall, and said that he had read of many priests and pharisees in the Bible who were far more guilty, because they had shed the blood of Christ.

At last the committal document was ready, and Bunyan was put in charge of the constable to be taken to prison. Meanwhile Bunyan's worried friends had been conferring together. Two of them met Bunyan on his way to the prison, and asked the constable to wait while they went to Wingate to plead for him. The constable agreed to wait—perhaps by now he was convinced of Bunyan's innocence—and after a time the friends hurried back with the message that if only Bunyan would say 'certain words' to the Justice, he might be released. Bunyan, perhaps pitying his friends, agreed to go with them, but said it was only on condition that the words could be said 'with a good conscience'.

Once more the little company walked back to Wingate's house, and Bunyan records that he lifted up his heart to God for light and strength from doing anything to dishonour him or to be a grief or discouragement to any who were followers of Jesus Christ.

Again he was taken into Wingate's house, but by now it was getting dark. After a little while a man came into the room, holding up a candle and peered at Bunyan in the flickering light.

'What, John Bunyan,' he said, apparently with great affection. Bunyan was amazed. He said later that he thought the man was about to 'leap on his neck' and kiss him. Bunyan felt sure this was a traitorous approach by a 'right Judas', and he was right. The man, William Foster, was a lawyer from Bedford, and was Wingate's brother-in-law. It may well have been that he was there because Wingate wanted to consult him on the legal position, so that somehow they could trap Bunyan. Bunyan knew him as 'a close opposer of the ways of God' and later he continually persecuted and harassed the Puritans.

Foster now pretended to have Bunyan's interests at heart, and said if only he would cease gathering people together he should have his liberty, for, he asserted, 'My brother-in-law is very loth to send you to prison, if you would only be ruled by him.' Bunyan replied that his business was only to exhort people to look after the salvation of their souls so that they might be saved. Foster pressed another argument, saying that only foolish and ignorant people ever listened to Bunyan. Bunyan replied sharply that it was the foolish and ignorant who had most need of teaching. Again Foster argued; again Bunyan replied that he dared not leave off the work which God had given him. Foster, seeing Bunyan could not be moved, finally left angrily.

More pressure was then put on him. Some of Wingate's servants were sent in, and told him their master was willing to let him go, if only he would no longer call the people together. Bunyan told them that there were more ways than one in which a man might be said to call people together; and as his preaching might be described in that way, he dare not say he would cease calling people together. At that Mr Foster told Bunyan that he must then be sent to prison. Bunyan had refused to be moved, and they saw 'he was at a point', as they put it. The committal or mittimus was put into the constable's hand, and Bunyan was taken away.

Bunyan left the house as courageously as he had faced his accusers. His own record of that moment, written later in prison under the title *A Relation of My*

Imprisonment, bears the stamp of a most heroic fortitude. He wrote, 'Verily as I was going forth of the
doors, I had much ado to forbear saying to them, that I
carried the peace of God along with me. But I held my
peace, and blessed be the Lord, went away to prison
with God's comfort in my poor soul.'

CHAPTER 10

The Prisoner

John Bunyan was taken by the constable to the County Gaol in Bedford which stood on the corner of Silver Street and High Street, only a street away from his home. Here he and members of Bedford Meeting had visited prisoners in former days, as an act of loving concern for the welfare of their souls. Now he found himself in that squalid building where men and women criminals and debtors and political prisoners shared the day-room, and went to two separate dungeons at night. To a young and vigorous man used to walking long distances in the open air, who delighted in the birds, the trees, the sunny fields and the natural scenery around him, the sudden and cruel limiting of his life to one dark and crowded room must have been a terrible ordeal. Someone who later visited him described it as 'an uncomfortable and close prison'.

Outside the prison, news spread of Bunyan's arrest and caused consternation to his wife and friends. They decided that at least they would try and get him out on bail, so some of 'the brethren' of the meeting made a journey to visit Mr Crompton, a young magistrate at Elstow who knew Bunyan. At first he was inclined to agree to their urgent request and to accept the sureties they offered; but he was perplexed because up to that time there had been no other arrest simply for preaching, and he thought there must be something more serious behind the charge. The charge on Bunyan's committal stated that he went about to several conventicles in Bedfordshire 'to the great disparagement of the Church of England'. Bunyan was taken to see the magistrate, who eventually refused the request to grant him bail.

Bunyan relates that he was not daunted by this disappointment, because before he saw the Justice he had begged God that if he would do more good by being set at liberty than by being in prison, then he might be set free. But if not, 'his will be done'. When he was back in prison, he said, 'I did meet my God sweetly in the prison again, comforting of mc and satisfying of me that it was his will and mind that I should be there.'

Bunyan, writing down his account of his imprisonment, finished the first part of it by describing the events up to this point with words which were a great testimony of faith, and an example of the remarkable courage of this great prisoner of conscience:

> Let the rage and malice of men be never so great, they can do no more, nor go farther than God permits them: But when they have done their worst, we know all things shall work together for good to them that love God.
>
> Farewell.

It seems as if Bunyan experienced joy in his heart because, like the early apostles, he was counted *worthy* to suffer for Christ. This fact transcended everything else in his mind. Nevertheless the state of his family caused him great anxiety, and his faith was greatly tested.

At home in St Cuthbert Street his wife Elizabeth, hardly more than a girl, and with four little children to look after, was expecting her first child. She later described with great poignancy what then happened:

> I was with child when my husband was first apprehended: but

being young and unaccustomed to such things, I being 'smayed at the news, fell into labour, and so continued for eight days, and then was delivered, but my child died.

Clearly she suffered greatly and must have been very frightened, but she was a brave and faithful young wife and later was to take action herself in a remarkable way.

The weeks passed slowly until January 1661 when the Quarter Sessions were held, and the time came for Bunyan to be taken before the Justices. Hopes were high that he might be released. He was brought before the magistrates and charged with having 'devilishly and perniciously abstained from coming to church to hear Divine Service', and for being 'a common upholder of several unlawful meetings and conventions, to the great disturbance and distraction of the good subjects of the Kingdom'.

Sir John Keeling, the Chairman of the Bench, was a harsh and sometimes brutal man. As a Royalist he had suffered under the Commonwealth, and he was bitterly hostile to Puritans. Of the other Justices, Sir Henry Chester was Francis Wingate's uncle. He, with Sir William Beecher, Sir George Blundell and Thomas Snagg, composed the Bench whom Bunyan had to face. All were implacably opposed to the Puritans, so there could be no impartiality in their judgement. They did, however, give Bunyan plenty of opportunity to speak, hoping, no doubt, that he would condemn himself by his own words. The charge was clearly unsatisfactory in every way as Bunyan had done nothing illegal. The Act of Uniformity, which virtually put an end to all Nonconformist or Puritan groups by making the Prayer Book compulsory in all English churches was not passed until 1662, a year later. After that, two thousand Puritan ministers who refused to conform, were ejected from their livings. It seems clear that if Bunyan had claimed leniency under Charles II's Declaration from Breda, the Justices would have needed to prove that his preaching endangered the peace and well-being of the realm—the one proviso against liberty for those of 'tender conscience'—and this of course they could not do.

Bunyan stood quietly before the Justices, who asked him what he had to say to the charge. He answered that he frequently attended the Church of God. Keeling pressed him on this point: 'Do you come to the parish church, to hear Divine Service?'

Bunyan answered that he did not.

'Why?' asked Keeling.

Bunyan said he did not find it commanded in the word of God. Keeling said that they were commanded to pray. This touched the very point on which Bunyan felt so strongly: 'But not by the Common Prayer-book,' he answered.

'How then?' said Keeling.

'With the Spirit,' Bunyan answered, 'as the Apostle saith, I will pray with the Spirit and with understanding.' It is interesting to note here that extempore or spontaneous prayer is still today one of the strongest features of worship in all Nonconformist churches, while the Prayer Book, (or The Alternative Service Book) contains the set form of services and prayers in all Anglican and Church of England worship.

Note

Keeling answered that we might pray with the Spirit and with understanding, and with the Common Prayer-book also. Bunyan now made a clear and direct statement of his unbreakable and unalterable belief. He later wrote down his reply: 'I said that those prayers in the Common Prayer-book was such as was made by other men, and not by the motions of the Holy Ghost within our hearts.'

Nothing could move him from this statement, although the Justices continued to examine him at length about his beliefs.

At last Keeling warned him: 'Let me give you one caution; take heed of speaking irreverently of the Common Prayer-book: For if you do so, you will bring great damage upon yourself.'

Bunyan, given liberty to speak, went on to give further reasons for not using the Prayer Book. His arguments were clearly becoming too difficult for the Justices. One said, 'He will do harm; let him speak no further.'

Keeling replied very impatiently, 'He can do no harm, we know the Common Prayer-book hath been ever since the Apostles' time, and is lawful to be used in church.'

This was, of course, a ridiculous and totally untrue statement as the Prayer-book then in use had been drawn up in 1552 under Edward VI. Justice Keeling was clearly becoming defeated by Bunyan's arguments.

They then began to attack him, saying he was deluded and possessed by the devil. Eventually, as Bunyan calmly and with determination pursued his argument, the Justices said they could give him no more time, adding quickly, 'You confess the indictment, do you not?'

Bunyan recounted later that at that moment he suddenly realized he had been indicted and found guilty. With dignity he then made a statement: 'I said, this I confess, we have had many meetings together, both to pray to God, and to exhort one another, and that we had the sweet comforting presence of the Lord among us for our encouragement, blessed be his name therefore. I confessed myself guilty no otherwise.'

The Justices had clearly heard enough. Impatient to end the case, Keeling said, 'You must be had back again to prison, and there lie for three months following; at three months end, if you do not submit to go to church to hear divine service, and leave your preaching, you must be banished the realm: And if, after such a day as shall be appointed you to be gone, you shall be found in this realm, or be found to come over again without special license from the king, you must stretch by the neck for it, I tell you plainly.'

'And so,' added Bunyan, 'he bid my gaoler have me away.'

In the face of this terrible sentence, Bunyan still had the dogged determination to make a last and almost defiant statement. He turned, and said that if he was freed from prison that very day, he would with the help of God, preach the gospel the next day.

The Justices were exasperated with him. The gaoler hastily pulled him away, and he never heard their reply. So he went back to prison, and there made a remarkable comment in the face of such disaster: 'I bless the Lord Jesus Christ...my heart was sweetly refreshed in the time of my examination, and afterwards at my returning to prison.'

The future for Bunyan now looked appalling. He faced three more long months in prison, and his family was destitute, forced to rely entirely upon the help of the loyal friends of Bedford Meeting. He had taken his stand on a matter of profound conviction and belief. Like Martin Luther, his conscience was captive to the word of God, and he could do no other. Yet he knew that if he held to his beliefs he could only look forward to transportation, with his family evicted from their home, and all his possessions sold. He himself might even be sold into some form of slavery overseas. Dreadful anxieties crowded in upon him, and in the most tragic and poignant words he ever wrote, he described his anguish:

> I found myself a man, and compassed with infirmities; the parting with my Wife and poor Children hath oft been to me in this place as the pulling of the flesh from my bones; and that not only because I am somewhat too fond of these great mercies, but also because I should have often brought to my mind the many hardships, miseries and wants that my poor family was like to meet with, should I be taken from them, especially my poor blind Child, who lay nearer my heart than all I had besides; O the thoughts of the hardship I thought my blind one might go under, would break my heart to pieces.

Then, as if in torment, he thought of what might become of his little blind Mary:

Poor child! thought I, what sorrow art thou like to have for thy portion in this world? Thou must be beaten, must beg, suffer hunger, cold, nakedness, and a thousand calamities, though I cannot now endure the wind should blow upon thee; but yet recalling myself, thought I, I must venture you all with God, though it goeth to the quick to leave you.

He felt he was pulling down his house and home over the heads of his wife and children, and destroying their life. Yet desperately clinging to his faith he wrote, 'I must do it, I must do it.'

As usual, in his grief he turned to the Bible, where he found some verses in the book of Jeremiah which he felt had been given to him to help him. One was strikingly apt: 'Leave thy fatherless children, I will preserve them alive, and let thy widows trust in me.' The other read, 'The Lord said, Verily it shall be well with thy remnant; verily I will cause the enemy to entreat thee well in the time of evil.'

It is interesting to realize that Bunyan, believing in the Bible as totally the inspired word of God to man—God's message to his people, as valid for the present as the past—was accustomed to apply texts to himself and his needs, particularly in times of testing, temptation or sorrow. Indeed, all through the ages men and women have got profound comfort from taking many of the thoughts and words of the Bible to themselves, appropriating them, as it were, to their needs, for comfort and inspiration and guidance. It is still a widespread custom today among Christians of all denominations, but perhaps particularly among those who are, in a sense, the descendants of the Puritans. They base their firm belief on the inspiration of the Scriptures, and hold to the apostle Peter's words referring to the prophetic writings of the Old Testament, 'holy men of God spake as they were moved by the Holy Ghost.'

So John Bunyan stood firm, but the haunting and terrible thought stayed with him that his life might end on the

Satan

gallows. He records that Satan 'Laid hard at me to beat me out of heart.' For he felt he really was not fit or ready to die. He pictured himself climbing up the ladder on to the scaffold to die, so desperately frightened that his stumbling legs would only make 'a scrabbling shift' at it, thus betraying his fears to all who stood and watched. He worried that he might faint from fear and that this would cause people to mock at his cowardice as a Christian, 'For,' he wrote, 'I was ashamed to die with a pale face, and tottering knees, for such a Cause as this.'

His active and colourful imagination tortured him: he even felt the rope about his neck, and could only pray earnestly, desperately to God to comfort and strengthen him. He encouraged himself with the thought that he might have the opportunity to speak his very last words to the crowd who would come and see him die. If only he could convert one soul at that moment then he could say, 'I shall not count my life thrown away, nor lost.'

Yet fearful thoughts continued to torment him.

'Whither must you go when you die?'

'What will become of you?'

'Where will you be found in another world?'

After many weeks of such suffering, he came to realize that since it was for the word and the way of God that he was in prison, he would not flinch a hair's breadth from the stand he had taken. 'So,' he wrote, 'I am for going on, and venturing my eternal state with Christ.'

The next three months dragged on. Then unexpectedly Bunyan had a visit from Paul Cobb, the Clerk to the Justices, who explained he had come on behalf of the Justices to admonish him and to demand his submission to the Church of England. Cobb clearly had quite a kind concern for the obstinate young tinker who was in such terrible danger. Yet, like the Justices, he could not get the better of him in argument, and for every point Bunyan had a powerful answer. Bunyan maintained that the Law was for wrongdoers and not people like himself whose whole aim was to do good.

'But, goodman Bunyan,' said Cobb, 'cannot you submit, and, notwithstanding do as much good as you can in a neighbourly way, without having such meetings?'

Bunyan would not yield. The Lord had given him his gift of preaching. He dared not refuse to exercise it.

Cobb at last realized he was getting nowhere. He made one last plea: 'Well, neighbour Bunyan,' he said, 'but indeed I would wish you seriously to consider these things between this and the Quarter Sessions, and to submit yourself. You may do much good if you continue still in the land. But alas, what benefit will it be to your friends, or what good can you do them, if you should be sent away beyond the seas into Spain, or Constantinople, or some other remote part of the world. Pray be ruled.'

At this point the gaoler, who had developed a real liking for Bunyan, could not resist joining in: 'Indeed, Sir,' he said, 'I hope he will be ruled.'

Cobb then got up to go, and Bunyan later wrote, 'I did thank him for his civil and meek discoursing with me; and so we parted. O! that we might meet in Heaven.'

Sympathetic up to a point as Cobb certainly was, he could not take Bunyan's views seriously, and, like the Justices, he still saw him as an ignorant young tinker. In point of fact Bunyan's remarkable intelligence was far superior to that of his accusers. He possessed a brilliance of mind that left them far behind, and would one day carry his name across the world.

CHAPTER 11

Elizabeth

In all John Bunyan's writings there is only one occasion where his wife Elizabeth figures prominently in the story, although one senses that she kept the little family together with indomitable courage while he was in prison. But on this occasion she holds the centre of the stage and she holds it alone. In *A Relation of My Imprisonment* there is ✓ a very careful account of all that occurred.

1661

In April 1661 thousands of prisoners were to be released as an act of clemency to mark King Charles II's coronation. Elizabeth and Bunyan's friends had prayed that he would be set free at this time, particularly in view of the King's Declaration of Liberty to those of tender conscience. But the names of those to be released had to be put forward by the local authority, and in Bedford the authorities were extremely hostile to the 'troublesome tinker', as they thought of him. Consequently Bunyan's name was not submitted, and on the day of the great release of prisoners he was still in prison. On that day there was a tremendous thunderstorm, and Bunyan could well have felt that it symbolized the storm in his own life.

Now the gaoler, who was sorry for Bunyan, used to allow Elizabeth to visit him in prison. This enabled them to work out a plan.

First, Bunyan had to prepare a petition asking for his

release. Then Elizabeth had to do what was a very daring thing for so young and inexperienced a girl. She had to make the long journey—as it was then—to London to present the petition to the Earl of Bedford.

This must have seemed a tremendous task, but she set out with great hopes. She saw the Earl, who consented, apparently sympathetically, to present the petition in the House of Lords, and he took it himself. Their reply was not at all unfavourable. They said that it was not in their power to release Bunyan but they recommended that the judges set him free at the next Assizes.

Bunyan's hopes rose. He prayed that he might at last get a fair trial. But then he found he was not even to be sent forward for an open trial.

While Bunyan prayed, Elizabeth went by herself to the Midsummer Assizes and presented the petition to one of the judges, Sir Matthew Hale, who was said to be lenient to dissenters and Puritans, and who had come to Bedford on circuit that year. He received her kindly but told her that although he would do what he could he feared it would come to nothing.

The next day the other Assize judge, Judge Twysden, was driving through Bedford in his carriage. In a moment of desperate determination Elizabeth ran out to where he was passing by in St Paul's Square, ran along beside the carriage, and threw the petition in at its window. Judge Twysden picked it up angrily and told her that it was no use, her husband could not be released until he promised not to preach.

Elizabeth had no intention of giving up. She was determined to fight with all her strength for her husband's freedom. She went to the Court-house, pushed her way through the crowds, and when there was a pause in the business of the court she went forward to face Sir Matthew Hale again. He, it is known, was a good and Christian man. He turned to her kindly, seeing her great distress. But near him was Sir Henry Chester, one of the magistrates before whom Bunyan had earlier appeared. He told the Judge that the Justices had properly convicted him, that he was a hot-spirited fellow, and the case was closed. Sir Matthew Hale rather sadly sent her away.

Still Elizabeth would not give up. She next went to see the High Sheriff, Edmund Wylde, of Houghton Conquest. He spoke kindly to her and suggested she should make one last effort for her husband. He told her to go to the Swan Chamber in the Swan Inn when the Assizes were over as the Judges would be gathering there before leaving town. This was a terrible ordeal, but she bravely made her way there, to find the room crowded with Justices, the local gentry of the County, and the Judges. In such a company she felt quite alone and frightened. Bunyan later described how his poor wife went into the room 'with a bashed [abashed] face, and a trembling heart'.

Very nervously she turned to Judge Hale. 'My Lord,' she said, 'I make bold to come once again to your Lordship to know what may be done with my husband.'

This time Judge Hale, perhaps startled at her sudden appearance, spoke firmly to her: 'Woman, I told thee before I could do thee no good; because they have taken that for a conviction which thy husband spoke at the Sessions: And unless there be something to undo that, I can do thee no good.'

Elizabeth would not give in, and pressed her point. 'My Lord, he is kept unlawfully in prison,' she said. 'They clap'd him up before there were any proclamation against the meetings; the indictment is also false: Besides they never asked him if he was guilty or no; neither did he confess the indictment.'

One of the Justices then broke in, obviously angry at the suggestion of injustice. 'My Lord, he was lawfully convicted.'

Elizabeth bravely stood her ground. 'It is false,' she said, 'for when they said to him, do you confess the indictment? He said only this, that he had been at several meetings, both where there was preaching the word, and prayer, and that they had God's presence among them.'

Judge Twysden then grew very angry, saying Bunyan was a breaker of the peace, and was convicted by the Law. But Judge Hale was now determined to get to the root of the matter, and see justice done. He called for the Statute Book.

'My Lord, he was not lawfully convicted,' Elizabeth repeated.

At this Sir Henry Chester, the magistrate became most annoyed and impatient, and kept on repeating, 'It is recorded, it is recorded,' as he tried to stop her speaking.

At this point Elizabeth made quite a long and a remarkably clear speech to Judge Hale, recounting how the Earl of Bedford had presented Bunyan's petition to the House of Lords, who said it was not in their power to release him, but they committed his release to the Judges at the next Assize. She went on, growing bolder as she spoke: 'Now I come to you to see if anything may be done in this business, and you give neither releasement nor relief.'

At this the Judges did not answer, but Sir Henry Chester still kept on saying, 'It is recorded.' Then he burst out into a rage, 'My Lord, he is a pestilent fellow, there is not such a fellow in the country again.'

Judge Twysden turned to Elizabeth and asked her if her husband would stop preaching. 'If he will do so, send for him.'

At this poor Elizabeth had nothing left to plead except to defend Bunyan's stand. 'My Lord, he dares not leave preaching as long as he can speak.' She went on to say he only wanted to live peaceably, and to follow his calling so that he could support his family. Then poignantly she added: 'My Lord, I have four small children, that cannot help themselves, of which one is blind, and have nothing to live upon, but the charity of good people.'

Judge Hale looking at her, for she was little more than a girl, asked immediately how one so young could have four children. With great pathos she explained she had only been married two years, and was their stepmother, and she told of the loss of her own first child at the time of Bunyan's arrest.

'Alas, poor woman,' said Judge Hale compassionately.

But Judge Twysden cruelly remarked that she made poverty her cloak, and he believed Bunyan was better supported by 'running up and down and preaching' than by following his calling.

'What is his calling?' asked Judge Hale and some of the people in the room shouted out, 'A tinker, my Lord.'

At this Elizabeth broke in with anger and hurt at their scorn: 'Yes, and because he is a tinker, and a poor man, therefore he is despised and cannot have justice.'

There is no doubt that Judge Hale not only had sympathy for her, but did suspect that Bunyan's conviction of guilt by the magistrates might not have been a right judgement. He said very kindly and without rebuking her, that she should do one of three things—apply to the King, or 'sue out a pardon', or get a writ of error. These words, suggesting a possible miscarriage of justice, infuriated Sir Henry Chester, who angrily declared that Bunyan would go on preaching and would do whatever he liked.

'He preacheth nothing but the word of God,' Elizabeth responded.

Judge Twysden then got into such a rage that Elizabeth thought he was going to strike her. 'He preach the word of God,' said the Judge scornfully. 'He runneth up and down and doth harm.'

'No, my Lord,' said Elizabeth. 'It's not so, God hath owned him and done much good by him.'

Twysden furiously replied that Bunyan's teaching came from the devil.

Elizabeth faced a roomful of hostile and angry people, all important in their own way in Courts, in public service, or through owning land and property. She stood there, the young tinker's wife, destitute and friendless, and yet she gave her response with a grave and touching dignity: 'My Lord, when the righteous Judge doth appear, it will be known that his doctrine is not of the devil.'

Twysden began to shout, 'My Lord do not mind her; send her away.'

Judge Hale, the only person in the room who showed any sympathy to Elizabeth, refused to treat such a brave young woman contemptuously. He repeated his instruction to her, and ended by saying that to get a writ of error would be the cheapest course of action for her. This hint of dissatisfaction at the magistrates' decision infuriated Sir Henry Chester.

Elizabeth made one last desperate plea—that they let her husband speak for himself, for he would do it so much better than she could. When this failed, and she had obtained no success in her brave mission, she burst into tears, worn out with the strain of her great ordeal. But it was more than that, and what she finally said shows that she totally shared her husband's strong faith. She was crying, she said, not only for the unkindness shown to her and her husband, but for the thought of the sad account such poor creatures would have to give at the Second Coming of their Lord, when they would have to answer for all their deeds.

So Bunyan remained in prison that long winter. When in 1662 the Spring Assizes came, he tried yet again to have his case brought to the Court. But the Justices and Mr Cobb, the Clerk to the Justices, managed cunningly to have his name withdrawn from the list of cases, and Bunyan recorded: 'Thus was I hindered and prevented at that time also from appearing before the Judge: and left in Prison. Farewell.'

CHAPTER 12

The Writer

After the total failure of the petition so bravely but unsuccessfully presented by his wife, John Bunyan faced an indefinite term of imprisonment. His future looked indescribably bleak. Yet even he could not have dreamed that he would have to be a prisoner for twelve long years. At first he had to live among criminals and even mad people, but soon he was joined by many more prisoners of conscience. When Parliament passed the Act of Uniformity in 1662 making the use of the Prayer Book compulsory in all churches, two thousand Puritan ministers who refused to conform were turned out of their livings, and Bunyan was joined by friends and fellow sufferers.

John Doe, a comb-maker of London, who was later to write a biographical sketch of Bunyan's life, went to visit the prison, and found more than sixty Dissenters and Puritans in prison with him. As a result, he said, the prison was grossly overcrowded. The prisoners included some fellow-members of the Bedford Meeting, and in one way Bunyan must have been thankful to be joined by them and to share fellowship with them once more.

Among the prisoners were ministers ejected from their churches, including a certain John Donne, Rector of Pertenhall, who, after the ejection, bravely used to gather his people together for worship by night in a secret place in

His life had shrunk to the confines of the prison; yet forbidden to preach, he could still write (page 103).

Keysoe Wood. This practice ended dramatically when constables, probably alerted by paid informers or spies, arrested the whole company, and sixty people were rounded up and taken to Bedford County gaol.

Now there was a real congregation of Christians, who suddenly found themselves together in dire circumstances. Bravely they gathered regularly to worship God, to read the Bible, to pray and to preach in turn. The prison day-room temporarily became a chapel, and here, as Bunyan later recorded, he felt the presence of the Lord with him. One fellow-prisoner, John Wilson, wrote a description of Bunyan: 'I have heard Mr Bunyan both preach and pray with that mighty spirit of faith...that has made me stand and wonder.'

When it was Bunyan's turn to preach, he clearly spoke with great power, and some of his sermons seem to have suggested an outline for the books and pamphlets which rapidly began to come from his pen in prison. For in that dismal place he was free to exercise both his gifts: preaching and writing.

Bunyan had no library of books from which to study, yet he did have a 'library', described by a visiting friend as 'the least and yet the best that ever I saw'. It consisted of Foxe's Book of Martyrs and the Bible. Bunyan drew great inspiration from the lives of those who suffered to the end for faith in Christ, but it was in the Bible that he steeped himself. Its beauty of language, the nobility and inspiration of its thought, and the majestic words of comfort, consolation and encouragement, inspired and sustained him. There, too, tragedy and triumph went side by side. The great promises rang through his mind like a peal of bells. The words became part of himself; often he thought and wrote in the language of the Bible, yet his words also contained the plain direct language and the vivid and often earthy speech of the common people.

There was something about Bunyan that had a deep influence on other prisoners. His calm courage, his steadfast character, the power in him that was tempered by suffering, the discipline of controlled grief, all combined to make this young brazier impressive to watch. John Wilson wrote:

> His countenance was grave and sedate, and did so to the life discover the inward frame of his heart, that it was convincing to the beholders, and did strike something of awe into them that had nothing of the fear of God.

The high-spirited adventurous boy, the ringleader in sports and every imaginable kind of game, the boy who loved dancing so much that it nearly broke his heart to give it up, who rang the church bells so happily, who so often played the 'madman', had become a man whose suffering revealed his greatness. He had been terribly tested, mocked at, cruelly deprived of freedom, and his life had shrunk to the confines of the prison; yet within it he set about building a new life, and counting the old life as dead. He had become a valiant soldier for Jesus Christ.

At this time he was extremely worried about his family, and set about making a huge quantity of 'tagg'd laces' (bootlaces) to earn a little money to help support them, for they were quite destitute, and Bedford Meeting people were not wealthy, although those who were not sent to prison did what they could to help. He also carved a flute from the leg of his prison stool to make music in that gloomy place.

There is no doubt that the gaoler was not only impressed by his fortitude, but wanted to help him, and since he was not a common criminal Bunyan managed to persuade the gaoler to let him leave prison occasionally. He was allowed to have food brought, and little Mary regularly came with soup for him.

For a short period between the Autumn Assizes of 1661 and the Spring Assizes of 1662 he was granted snatches of freedom. At that time he was urgently trying

Little blind Mary regularly took soup to him in prison (page 104).

to get his name on the calendar of prisoners for trial and probably both he and the sympathetic gaoler expected he might be released. Bunyan records that 'Between these two Assizes I had by my Jailer, some liberty granted me, more than at the first, and how I followed my wonted course of preaching, taking all occasions that was put into my hand to visit the people of God.' Perhaps he quietly slipped into his home to see his wife and children; and there was one thing he would *not* stop doing as he had said to the judges. He went secretly to meet the poor bewildered people of Bedford Meeting to preach to them and to encourage them to be steadfast in the faith of Jesus Christ. He was, indeed, reckless about this, regarding himself as under orders from the Lord, and the end to this brief freedom came when on one occasion, no doubt hearing of the persecution of the Dissenters and Puritans in London, he left the prison for a day or two, 'to see the Christians at London'. This bold and daring act proved disastrous. He recounts what happened in his book *A Relation of My Imprisonment*:

I...did go to see Christians at London, which my enemies hearing of, was so angry, that they had almost cast my Jailor out of his place, threatening to indite him, and to do what they could against him. They charged me also, that I went thither to plot and raise division, and make insurrection, which, God knows, was a slander; whereupon my liberty was more straitened than it was before; so that I must not look out of the door.

A small contemporary drawing shows him fettered by a long chain.

Once more deprived of all liberty, intensely energetic by character, with a mind that was ceaselessly active, and an imagination so vivid that it invested all that happened with drama and colour, he turned again to writing small tracts which perhaps brought in a little

1663

income to help his family.

Christian Behaviour, published in 1663, was the third of his enlarged sermons, as they might be described, to come from his pen in prison. This was a kind of personal testament concerned with Christian relationships and duties. These included admirable and, for those days, enlightened instructions to parents urging them to show gentleness and kindness.

This book also contains a very beautiful picture in words, and here Bunyan the poet is seen:

> Christians are like the several flowers in a garden, that have upon each of them the dew of heaven, which, being shaken with the wind, they let fall their dew at each other's roots, whereby they are jointly nourished, and become nourishers of each other.

This book was written while he still expected that he might be sent to the gallows, and he writes in it movingly,

> Thus have I, in few words, written to you before I die, a word to provoke you to faith and holiness, because I desire that you may have the life that is laid up for all them that believe in the Lord Jesus, and love one another, when I am deceased.

Bunyan also wrote works of poetical dialogue, meditations and tracts from prison. One treatise was called *Praying in the Spirit*, and this is a sort of manifesto of his reasons for refusing to use the Book of Common Prayer. He describes the authorities who force it on people as 'hot for the form and not for the power of praying'. He is very angry that men leading most dissolute lives should be counted upright and honest because they came to church and said 'Our Father', while those like him who were not willing to follow 'vain traditions' but who wanted to worship God and pray spontaneously in spirit and in truth were looked upon as the enemies of God and of the nation. He adds bitterly: 'I trow you will find those that plead for the spirit of prayer in the jail, and them that look after the form of men's inventions only in the alehouse.'

Another work, *Prison Meditations* appeared in 1665 and is a kind of reply to a friend who had written to him in prison encouraging him to '*keep his head above the flood*'. Bunyan replies in verse, and says that although he is in prison, his mind is free:

> For though men keep my outward man
> Within their bolts and bars,
> Yet by the faith of Christ, I can
> Mount higher than the Stars.

It seems likely that shortly after this Bunyan began to write *Grace Abounding to the Chief of Sinners*, a spiritual autobiography in the style of a 'testimony', or declaration of God's dealings with his soul. It is a classic of spiritual writing, and the experiences contained in it were later transformed into the dramatic allegory and imaginative fiction of *The Pilgrim's Progress*. The Puritans, particularly, liked to use such a testimony of conversion to strengthen the faith of others and to encourage those who had not come to faith in Christ. Indeed, in many or most of their gatherings, as in Bedford Meeting, new members were encouraged to give an account of their journey to faith. Bunyan would have recounted his story to them, and this book is almost certainly a development from that. It is interesting to note that today there is a great demand for, and sale of, popular Christian autobiographies and biographies. In the end personal witness is far more effective than any amount of theologizing. However, few if any present day books, come up to the standard of this intensely personal and wonderfully vivid work of Bunyan.

This book was printed in London in 1666 by George Larkin. Bunyan's previous works had been printed by a certain Francis Smith who, because his place of business was at the Elephant and Castle in London, near Temple Bar, was known as 'Elephant Smith'. But he was an Anabaptist, and by 1666 was also in prison for his publications. His contemporaries described him as 'a man of great sincerity and happy contentment in all walks of life', and yet like Bunyan he had to undergo much suffering, and the seizure of his books including those of Bunyan. Many, if not all of these are thought to have been destroyed in the Fire of London.

The two great disasters that struck London from 1665–1666 were the Great Plague and the Great Fire. Thousands died through the Plague which spread into various places in the country and even raged around Bedford Gaol. This was followed by the Great Fire, a catastrophe for which there was no parallel in the long history of London. It blazed fiercely for five days, destroying the whole of the City between the Tower and the Temple.

During this time of disorganization and disaster, some person or persons pleaded for Bunyan's release. This was recorded by Charles Doe who recounts that Bunyan was given a short spell of liberty in 1666 'by the intercession of some interest or power that took pity on his sufferings'. His period of freedom was short. Bunyan had still one aim: to witness to his Lord to all who would listen. He went back yet again to preaching. Doe simply states that 'A little after his release they took him again at a meeting, and put him in the same gaol where he lay six years more.'

Few details of this event are known. Bunyan says that when the constable came to take him, he was just about to preach on the subject, 'Dost thou believe on the Son of God?' Bunyan, with his open Bible in his hand, then fixed his eyes upon the constable who turned pale, and let go his hold upon him and stood back, at which Bunyan exclaimed, 'See how this man trembles at the word of God.'

It is now generally thought that somewhere about this time, between 1666 and 1672, Bunyan began to create his greatest and most remarkable work, *The Pilgrim's Progress*. It appears that when thinking about another book the great drama began to unfold in his mind of the journey of Christian to the Heavenly City. Ideas started to pour into his mind. Great scenes began to be enacted and his excitement grew as

> In more than twenty things, which I set down;
> This done, I twenty more had in my Crown.

The story carried him out of himself, right out of the confines of the prison. He was a pilgrim travelling on a hazardous journey, having undertaken an enterprise so vital, so enthralling, that he was lost to the world. At first he says he wrote to please himself. He put pen to paper with delight; the story flowed. 'Still as I pull'd, it came; and so I penn'd it down.' He sets its beginning right where he is, in 'a Den' or prison; 'As I walked through the wilderness of this world I lighted upon a certain place where there was a Den, and I laid me down in that place to sleep; and as I slept I dreamed a dream.' He was now not writing out of the driving compulsion to preach, but out of the sheer enjoyment and fascination of his story, and for that reason he could, as it were, relax, and let it flow, never realizing then that when completed it would preach more power-fully and eloquently than any straight sermon.

The long slow years passed, and only two books were actually published by Bunyan during this second long term of imprisonment: his *Confession of Faith*, and, *A Defence of the Doctrine of Justification by Faith*, which was written at speed shortly before his release. The reason for this slowing down of his writing is not known. Was it because he could not get his writings licensed, and his original publisher, Francis Smith, was now too carefully watched to continue publishing unlicensed books? Or was it that the seemingly endless time in prison had caused a weariness of mind and spirit? If, as leading authorities now think, he was busy at this time creating *The Pilgrim's Progress*, then that may have been the reason, and he may have been deeply involved in it to the exclusion of other writing.

By 1668 it seems that the strictness of Bunyan's imprisonment was somewhat relaxed. It is likely that his gaolers had been cruel and oppressive through the years but a new gaoler 'took such pity on his rigorous suffering, that he put all care and trust into his hands'. In this year there was a gradual relenting towards Dissenters. The Bedford Church Book which had no entries in it after 1663, began to be kept again in 1668. The Conventicle Act of 1664 which had passed severe penalties on all attending Nonconformist 'conventicles' or meetings, expired in 1688. Although it was about to be renewed, it never actually was at that time, as Parliament was adjourned by the king's desire and it was seventeen months before it met again. During that brief breathing-space the Puritans enjoyed more liberty than they had done for five years.

From then on Bunyan's name begins to appear in the Bedford Church Book. Clearly he was once more allowed out for very brief periods; perhaps he then visited members of the meeting, particularly those who had lapsed. He was always one of the signatories to letters of exhortation, encouragement or rebuke to various members, and perhaps such letters were brought to him in prison for his approval and agreement. This greater freedom occurred before the final storm against the Puritans when the New Conventicle Act was passed by Parliament after the seventeen months break. This Act was described by the poet Andrew Marvell as the 'quintessence of arbitrary malice', and was more severe even than the Act of 1664.

An 'Illegal Conventicle' was now defined as any meeting for worship other than according to the practice of the Church of England, and if more than four people attended such meetings, whether in houses, fields, or any other uninhabited places, they were to be fined with great severity. One third of the fine was to go to any informer and his assistants. Magistrates and constables were empowered to break open doors, and the militia, with horse and foot soldiers could disperse such assemblies if necessary. This new attempt to suppress all Puritan and Nonconformist meetings, met with stiff and courageous opposition.

One such occurrence concerned Bedford Meeting. Twenty-eight of the congregation were discovered meeting secretly at the house of John Fenne, a haberdasher, and maker of hats. As a result, he appeared in court, and it was ordered that all his possessions were to be sequestered or seized. This incensed the Bedford people who were sympathetic to him, and to the Puritans. Following this, a certain Thomas Battison, the church warden of St Paul's and other officers were sent to collect the fines which had been imposed by the magistrate, Mr Foster, on those at the meeting who did not attend church. They went first to the home of one John Bardolph, who owned a malt-house. But the people were so infuriated that 'a great number of all sorts of persons were gathered about them, expressing by turns their indignation against him [Battison] for attempting this against Bardolph, whom the whole Town knew to be a just and harmless man; and the common sort of people covertly fixing a Calves tayl to Battison's back, and deriding him with shouts and hollows, he departed...' without getting the fines!

The records of this and other events were found in a pamphlet, published in 1670, entitled *A True and Im-*

*partial Narrative of some Illegal and Arbitrary Proceedings
by certain Justices of the Peace and others, against several
innocent and peaceable Nonconformists in and near the
Town of Bedford.*

But by this time the situation in the country was
beginning to change. Charles II had concluded the
Treaty of Dover, by which, in return for 'protection'
from the French, and in the hope of destroying the
power of the Dutch who had been in open hostility with
England, he declared himself a Roman Catholic at heart,
and promised to re-establish the Catholic religion in
England. Although his sympathy to the Roman Catholics was not made public, he desired to obtain religious
tolerance for them and, he said, to change 'the present
state of religion in England for a better'. He knew he
could not possibly do this unless he first obtained religious tolerance for the Dissenters. He therefore paved
the way by exercising his prerogative in an unconstitu-
tional way. He issued a Declaration of Indulgence,
which suspended the laws against both Dissenters and
Roman Catholics.

It was clear that there was at long last toleration for
the Nonconformists. Chapels began to be opened,
ministers started to return to their often dispersed congregations. Bunyan was still in prison in 1671 when,
seeing his freedom in sight, the members of Bedford
Meeting met together, with the intention of seeking
God 'about the choyce of bro. Bunyan to the office of
elder'. This was confirmed in the December.

In January 1672 the following record appears in the
Church Book:

> After much seeking God by prayer, and sober conference
> formerly had, the Congregation did at this meeting with
> joynt consent (signified by solemn lifting up of their
> hands), call forth and appoint our bro. Bunyan to the
> pastorall office or eldership: And he, accepting thereof,

gave up himself to serve Christ, and his Church in that charge; and received of the elders the right hand of fellowship.

1672 Bunyan, now officially Pastor of the Meeting, came out of prison in 1672 under the general pardon to the Quakers. He had gone into prison a young man, he came out middle-aged.

Yet of those terrible years he could say:

I never had in all my life so great an inlet into the Word of God as now. The Scriptures that I saw nothing in before are made in this place to shine upon me. Jesus Christ also was never more real and apparent than now. Here I have seen him and felt Him indeed.

CHAPTER 13

The Pastor

John Bunyan came home from prison in 1672 to a house full of children. Elizabeth had had a daughter Sarah, probably born about 1667, as it seems likely that she was conceived during Bunyan's very brief period of freedom in 1666. A son Joseph, who was to be his sixth and youngest child, was born during his first year of freedom.

As a Puritan, Bunyan looked on each of his children as a gift from God, and his love for them was always deepened by his belief that it was his solemn duty and privilege to bring them up 'in the fear of the Lord', a phrase much used at the time, and long after. So it was his task to teach them, and to nurture them in the Christian faith. A friend of his wrote that he was like Joshuah in the Bible who declared 'as for me and my house we will serve the Lord'. The same friend wrote that in his home 'he kept up a very strict discipline', and this may well have been because he greatly feared his children might 'fall into sin' as easily as he felt he had done as a boy. However, Charles Doe, in his biography of Bunyan, notes that he was indulgent to his children almost to a fault, and one glimpses behind those words the father who could enter into his children's play with all the high spirits and zest for enjoyment he had shown as a boy.

In all Puritan households, the Bible was the charter for

life. It was usually read morning and evening to the family from earliest years. The children though probably restless, would nevertheless almost unconsciously retain in their minds the beauty of its language, the majestic prose, the poetry of the Psalms, the solemn warnings of the prophets, and the great drama of the Gospels, and their thought patterns would be indelibly influenced and moulded for good.

Above all else, the children were taught that they had to make a solemn choice either to follow Christ or to reject him; to inherit eternal life, or to take the other terrible way that leads to destruction. This choice was theirs alone. It formed the great and ultimate purpose of life, and put a burden of responsibility on them.

Perhaps it sounds over-solemn, even stifling, to regard children as a sacred trust, as was the custom in Puritan families, and still is among their spiritual descendants. The fact remains that many such families remained loyal, close and happy units. Primarily this was because there was a strong sense of stability, and security in a settled family life, where there was so often an enfolding and caring love and concern for each member. It is true that sometimes the ceaseless concern for their souls' welfare weighed too heavily on over-sensitive children. Sometimes parents tried to drive children into the kingdom of heaven with the whip of fear and warnings of judgement and eternal separation from God for the unrepentant sinner, instead of with 'cords of love'—a far more effective means. In all families there were often rebels, although they not infrequently tended in the end to become the finest Christians. But Puritan families in Bunyan's time were often large, and the strictness was counter-balanced in many cases by the fun and laughter of the children who were not lonely and who played together and made their own amusements. Such solemnity in the home, as there was in Bunyan's time, was, however, heightened by the fragility of life, by the easy spread of disease, and the dangers of childbirth, so that parents thought it even more urgent that the children 'belonged to the Lord'.

In general, the Puritans worked exceedingly hard, believing all work must be honouring to God, and therefore should be carried out as well as possible. Many prospered because of this, and, indeed, in later years became great philanthropists. Those who today decry the Puritan work ethic should remember that it bred people of enormously strong character as well as great talents.

The relationship between husband and wife was, at its best, loving and faithful, for it was a permanent bond, never questioned, but entered on for life, for better or worse. It is a fact that there was a gentleness and serenity in many Puritan homes, and an enjoyment of the marriage relationship, that has never been fully recognized or understood by those outside their number, who tended then and now to regard them as narrow-minded and prejudiced. For Puritans, as for Catholics, the belief that 'the family that prays together, stays together', was the bedrock of life.

It is a very interesting fact that even in the early part of this century in the Church of Scotland, a Reformed Church, still with strong influences from the time of Calvin and John Knox, the 'children of the Manse' were statistically found to surpass all other groups in talent and high ability. This in no way stemmed from a background of wealth. Often the family income was comparatively very low, and the parents had to encourage the utmost thrift and care in the spending of every penny. It is not simply imaginative to think that the same was the case in Bunyan's time.

John Bunyan's home in St Cuthbert Street was small and unpretentious. Here he came home from prison to live very simply. When he was freed he found his business affairs had gone 'to wreck'. He was an independent man, and believed that it was right to continue in his craft as brazier, just as Paul was a tent-maker, rather than becoming dependent on others. In this way he could support his family and no doubt he trained up his older sons in the work. He was a real craftsman, and at one point he actually made a beautiful violin. Some money, probably not much, was coming in from his books, but he continued to live with no ostentation. His house had three small rooms on the ground floor, and an attic with a dormer window in the high-pitched tiled roof. Behind the house was an outbuilding which was his workshop. A picture of the simplicity of his home is given in the diary of an Oxford antiquary, Thomas Hearne, a contemporary of Bunyan's. Hearne records that a certain Mr Bayford, who was known to him, went to visit Bunyan, anxious to see the study of the great preacher and writer, expecting to find it full of books. He found the study contained hardly more than Bunyan had possessed in prison. There was just his Bible and a few copies of his own works on a shelf.

Bunyan must have shared deeply in the intense joy of the people of Bedford Meeting as he took up his duties as their pastor. He was granted a license from the government to act as a preacher in the house of Josias Roughead. This 'house' was a barn in an orchard in Mill Lane, Bedford, which Josias Roughead (or Ruffhead) had purchased from Mr Justice Crompton of Elstow. This was eventually bought by Bunyan for the Bedford Meeting for £50. Here Bunyan gathered his congregation and with great joy they once more met together in freedom to worship God. He began to preach and to teach, and so many people came to hear him that there was not even room for them. Seeing this, he consulted with his people about turning the barn into a proper meeting-house. They were very pleased with the idea and although many were poor, they all cheerfully made voluntary contributions.

When he preached there for the first time it was recorded that 'the place was so thronged that many were constrained to stay without, though the house was very spacious, everyone striving to partake of his instructions, that were of his persuasion, and show their good will towards him by being present at the opening of the place.' For the last intensely busy sixteen years of his life—with one break when he was once more imprisoned for about six months —this was the very centre of all his activity. However, his influence stretched far beyond it.

Not only had he applied for and obtained a license to preach in Josias Roughead's barn, but he had also himself applied for licenses for twenty-five other preachers, and thirty other buildings, in Northamptonshire, Buckinghamshire, Cambridgeshire and Hertfordshire, as well as nineteen places in Bedfordshire. The application for these licenses in Bunyan's own handwriting was preserved in the Record Office, together with hundreds of similar other applications. Upper rooms, private houses, malting-house floors, barns, gardens and even rooms in ruined monasteries and cellars in old castles were licensed for preaching places for the Puritans.

Bunyan was by now a towering figure among his own people, taking the oversight of villages far and near, preaching indefatigably whenever and wherever opportunity offered around the country. He is known to have preached in Leicester in 1672; and he also was welcomed by congregations in London. He became known affectionately as 'Bishop Bunyan'.

In prison John Bunyan had grown in compassion and in a deep sense of God's love, and this now showed in his preaching. Other characteristics emerged. In 1674 the Bedford Meeting Book records that 'Singing of Psalmes was proposed to the Congregation'. The man who had loved bell-ringing and dancing but had thought they must be sinful and unpleasing to God, had come to a peace of mind which enabled him to enjoy innocent and spontaneous pleasures with merriment. There is a lovely picture in the second part of *The Pilgrim's Progress* of a joyful celebration. One could almost imagine it might be a hint of what took place in Bunyan's home when he was freed from prison:

Now Christiana, if need be, could play upon the viol, and her daughter Mercy upon the lute. So, since they were so merry disposed, she played them a lesson, and Ready-to-halt would dance. So he took Despondency's daughter, named Much-afraid, by the hand, and to dancing they went in the road. True, he could not dance without one crutch in his hand, but I promise you, he footed it well; also the girl was to be commended, for she answered the music handsomely.

As for Mr Despondency, the music was not much to him, he was for feeding rather than dancing, for that he was almost starved. So Christiana gave him some of her bottle of spirits for present relief, and then prepared him something to eat; and in a little time the old gentleman came to himself and began to be finely revived.

So Bunyan went about his pastoral work with zest, able now to share both in his people's joys and sorrows, and that of course was biblical, for had not Paul said, 'Rejoice with them that rejoice, and weep with them that weep'? He had a very special love for people with troubles and sorrows, and did not spare himself in trying to get help for the poor and the destitute, and there were many. He particularly cared for the families of those who were prisoners of conscience, for he knew all too well the despair of those in that position. It was said of him at the time that he went to minister to any who were sick, and everywhere tried to bring peace and unity among Christians.

While he wanted nothing better than to preach the gospel, and to devote most of his time to this, he came face to face with various problems which greatly concerned him, and from time to time his pastorate was not easy. The man who had felt himself to be 'the Chief of Sinners' saved through grace, wanted to warn others in the strongest terms about falling into sin, and taking the pathway to death and destruction. It would appear he was scrupulous and unbending in this. Various entries in the Bedford Meeting Book record warnings and admonitions given to his flock:

July 14th, 1673, was to be 'kept as day of humiliation and praire upon several waighty accounts'. (Spellings in the entries are varied.)

Much more serious, it was recorded in another entry that the wife of Bro. Witt was 'cast out of the church... for railling, and other wicked practises'.

Sister Elizabeth Bigbie was severely rebuked 'for an immodest lieing in a chamber several nights wherein also lay a young man, nobody being in the house but them two'.

Sister Landy was reprimanded for 'withstanding communion again, for countenancing card-play, and for deceiving the Church with her former seeming repentance'.

Other members had run into debt, 'to the great dishonour of God and scandall of religion'.

In those last words Bunyan's fears and anxieties are crystallized. He and his fellow elders could not tolerate anything which might bring the Christian faith into disrepute. His strictness and enforcement of church discipline may have seemed harsh at times, yet it sprang from his intense desire that his people should worship God with pure hearts.

It seems likely that these problems were minor irritations in a ministry which was clearly bringing hundreds of people to listen and respond to God's message. He was greatly admired and looked up to as a fearless leader, a soldier of Christ, a strong man of great vitality and courage. He undoubtedly had a charisma that drew people to him as to a magnet.

Not a few in his position have, over the years, encountered difficult even disastrous situations arising from malicious slander. One event, totally unlooked for and unexpected, could even have ruined him. A young Puritan woman, wrote down a very remarkable and totally spontaneous account of what actually happened in a document entitled, *A Relation of the Life of Mrs Agnes Beaumont Written by Herself*. This paints a vivid picture of one young Puritan woman's life in those days. We see her on her father's farm, we see her devout and fervent religious feelings, and her great admiration of Bunyan which was a kind of emotional hero-worship.

In December 1672, Agnes Beaumont, a young woman of twenty-two, had been the first to be received into full membership of the meeting at Gamlingay after Bunyan had become pastor. Her name is the first, entered in his handwriting, in the Church roll. He spells it 'Agniss Behemont'. She was the daughter of a farmer who was a widower, and who had once been deeply moved by Bunyan's preaching. But some neighbour had jealously and maliciously turned him against Bunyan with lying and false tales. Agnes, however, remained totally loyal and faithful to the meeting, as did her brother and sister, and she developed an enormous admiration for such a great man, as she thought of him.

In February 1674, hearing Bunyan was coming over to preach in Gamlingay, she begged her father to let her go. He very unwillingly consented. She walked to her brother's home about a mile away to go with him and a party of others. It had been planned that she would travel with a certain John Wilson, but unfortunately he did not turn up. The winter roads were impassable on foot. Her brother and his wife were travelling together on one horse, but no others were available. She was in despair, and wrote, 'It cut me to the heart; and fearing I should not go, I burst into tears; for my brother had told me his horses were all at work.'

Suddenly John Bunyan appeared on horseback, riding towards Gamlingay. Agnes, greatly daring but desperate, begged him to carry her behind him to the meeting.

'No; I will not carry her,' Bunyan said firmly to her brother, knowing only too well the danger of village gossip and scandal.

Her brother then intervened, saying to Bunyan, 'If you do not carry her, you will break her heart.'

Bunyan answered, 'Your father will be grievous angry

He came just in time to see her riding off behind Bunyan (page 124).

if I should.'

At this Agnes intreated him again. 'I will venture that,' she said.

At last, seeing her grief, and urged by her brother, Bunyan, against his own wishes, relented. Perhaps he knew of her lonely life, with no mother, caring for a difficult father. He certainly knew of her simple but deep faith and her love of the meeting. She was lifted up on to his horse, and they set off.

Meantime, Agnes' father had followed her down the road to see who she was going to travel with and came just in time to see her riding off behind Bunyan. Furiously angry, he started to run down the rough road to pull her off the horse; but he was too late, and could not catch them up.

Agnes records that her heart swelled with pride at being carried by 'this servant of the Lord'. But before long they happened to pass a clergyman who knew them both, and he gazed very closely at them. Probably he disapproved of Bunyan's meeting, and of his refusal to worship in the Church of England. But now he had a real weapon against him.

The meeting itself and the powerful preaching sent Agnes into a state of ecstasy, but after it was over she had to face the problem of getting home. The only person who would help her was a young woman who was able to bring her to within a quarter of a mile of the farm. Then in the darkness and wet and cold Agnes walked the last part of the journey. She found the house locked and no light showing.

'It is I, Father, come home wet and dirty; pray let me in,' she called.

Her father shouted back, 'Where you have been all day, you may go at night.' He was in a rage and refused to open the door unless she promised never to go to Bunyan's meetings again. This she felt she could not possibly do. So, wrapped in her wet riding-clothes, she went into the barn, and spent the night there. Here she prayed fervently for Christ's help, for she was very much afraid of being alone in the dark. She wrote that some words of scripture came vividly to her: 'Beloved, think it not strange concerning the fiery trial which is to try you' (1 Peter 4:12, AV). She recorded with wonder that on that bitter night, 'I felt no cold, although the dirt was frozen on my shoes in the morning.'

Next morning her father still refused to let her in, and much distressed she walked to her brother's house and remained there until the following Sunday. She was in real anguish of mind about his refusal to have her home, and went back to call to him on several occasions. Once she went with her sister, who was very upset for her, and who begged for his mercy for Agnes, but it was in vain. Her father grew ever more furious, calling from the window, and threatening not to leave her a penny when he died. On one visit she asked him to let her have her precious Bible. This was refused and she returned to her sister, crying most bitterly.

Later she returned again, and finding the door slightly open, pushed it gently and was about to enter, when her father rushed to shut it, nearly trapping her leg in the door in his violence. She then went to a dense part of the woodland by the farm with 'a heart full of sorrow'. Another scripture verse came to her: 'Call unto me, and I will answer thee, and shew thee great and mighty things, which thou knowest not' (Jeremiah 33:3, AV). She stayed there so long that eventually one of her brother's men was sent to look for her. He could not find her, and her brother and sister in great anxiety came over to search for her. On finding her at last, her brother took her back to his home again. On the Sunday she went with him to the meeting, and on their return they called yet again at her father's farm. Her brother had urged her to make no promise not to attend the meeting, but now she was worn down with grief and anxiety, and by her father's cruel attitude. Eventually, against her will and her conscience, she said, 'Well, father, I will promise you never to go to a meeting again as long as you live, without your consent.'

At last, on hearing this, her father relented and let her in. But she felt guilt-stricken and shaken with misery. 'This was the Lord's day night; and a black night it was to me,' she recorded. Agnes was now told to make the supper and her father became quite affectionate towards her. The next day Agnes was still weeping at having made her terrible promise, and seeing her grief her father became at last very 'softened' towards her, and he himself grew distressed and was overcome with grief. She records that he 'wept like a child', and explained that what had upset him so greatly was her riding behind Bunyan.

That night her father went to bed apparently in perfect health. During the night he suddenly became desperately ill. He seemed to have some sort of seizure and a pain at his heart. Agnes, in great fear, made the fire up, and got him something warm to drink, but he became violently sick and faint, and as he was trying to get up he fell to the floor. Unable to lift him, and terrified, she rushed out of the house and ran a mile in the cold of a winter's night through deep snow to fetch her brother. He got up and came back at once with two of his men. They arrived just in time to witness the father's death.

The situation now took on the quality of a nightmare. The news of the death was quickly passed around. A certain Mr Farrow, my 'bitter enemy', Agnes described him, who was a rejected suitor of hers, came to enquire if her father was dead. 'It is no more than what I looked for,' he said. He began to broadcast all around that he was sure Agnes had poisoned her father, and that John Bunyan had procured the poison for her to do it. The clergyman who had seen them riding together was also busy circulating a scandalous rumour about an immoral relationship between Agnes and Bunyan.

The rumour spread to the town, the funeral was put off, and a surgeon was called in. He agreed that a coroner and jury should be summoned. Agnes readily acquiesced in this, saying to her very anxious and distressed brother, 'O, brother, blessed be God for a clear conscience,' but her brother had begun to fear that Agnes might lose her life as a convicted murderess.

Agnes then 'went to the Lord and prayed that he would appear in this fiery trial'. She wrote, 'I did not know how far God might suffer this man [Farrow] and the devil to go.'

She began to be greatly afraid of being burned to death as a murderess. Not only so, but she began to realize that Bunyan was also being grievously slandered. 'But,' she said, 'the Lord knew our innocency in this affair, both in thought, word and deed.'

Friends from Gamlingay came and prayed with her in the morning of the day the Coroner was due. She then went and prayed alone and begged that God would 'Carry me above the fears of men, devils, and death, and give me faith and courage to lift up my head before my accusers.' In the event she sat by the fire with some neighbours as the Coroner and Jury passed through the room to see her father's body. She recounts how marvellously calm she was kept. The Coroner then came back to warm himself by the fire, and looked steadfastly at her, shaking his head.

The Coroner's Court was held in her brother's house, and Mr Farrow, her accuser, was summoned. In the event, Mr Farrow's confused accusations were totally discounted and death was found to be due to natural causes. The Coroner treated Agnes with great compassion, when he heard of her ordeal and how she had been alone in the house with her dying father. He told Mr Farrow that he had 'defamed this young woman in this public manner, endeavouring to take away her good name, yea, her life also if you could', and declared that he now should make it his business to establish her reputation. He added, 'You had no need to add to her affliction and sorrow; and if you were to give five hundred pounds, it would not make amends.' Turning to Agnes, he said, 'Sweetheart, do not be daunted. God will take care of thy preferment and provide thee a husband, notwithstanding the malice of this man . . . thank God for this deliverance, and never fear but he will take care of thee.'

In spite of her innocence, rumours still flew about, including one that Mr Bunyan was a widower, and had advised Agnes to poison her father so that he might marry her. 'But this report rather occasioned mirth than mourning,' Agnes wrote, 'because Mr Bunyan, at the same time, had a good wife living.'

In reading Agnes Beaumont's account, we can catch glimpses of the great strain under which Bunyan lived and see how easily lies and slanders could arise. Agnes seems almost more pleased with her own calmness than deeply anxious for Bunyan's hurt, although she does refer to it briefly. Is there possibly a trace of spiritual pride as she describes her composed bearing and actions under the slanderous accusations? She certainly had not been as concerned for his reputation as for her desire to go to the meeting with him on his horse, and her very emotional hero-worship of the great Mr Bunyan shines through all she writes.

It seems possible that it was after this unhappy affair that John Bunyan made the very strong and frank denial of any sexual misconduct in his life, which appears in the 1688 edition of *Grace Abounding*:

> My Foes have missed their mark in this their shooting at me. I am not the man . . . And in this I admire the wisdom of God, that he made me shy of women from my first conversion until now . . . .
>
> I bind these lies and slanders to me as an ornament; it belongs to my Christian profession to be vilified, slandered, reproached, and reviled; and since all this is nothing else, as my God and my conscience do bear me witness, I rejoice in reproaches for Christ's sake.

CHAPTER 14

The Den

After barely three years of freedom, John Bunyan had to face yet more trouble. King Charles II's Declaration of Indulgence to Dissenters and Roman Catholics was withdrawn because of great pressure from the House of Commons. He had made the Declaration without Parliament's approval and members were furious that the king felt he could suspend the laws of the realm by what he termed his 'inherent power'. Feelings ran so high that Charles gave in, tearing off the Great Seal on it with his own hands it is said.

As a result there was a withdrawal of all licences for preachers, and it was stated that no conventicle or meeting now had 'any authority, allowances or encouragement from His Majesty'. This was a terrible blow to the Puritans, who had already suffered so greatly. Bunyan was again a marked man, and in Bedfordshire where many members of the Established Church of England had suffered under Cromwell, hostility to all the Nonconformists ran high.

Dr William Foster, 'that right Judas' as Bunyan had termed him, who had come up to Bunyan in Harlington Hall after his arrest 'making as if he would have leaped on his neck and kissed him', had become Chancellor of the Bishop of Lincoln (in whose diocese Bedford lay) and was also Commissary of the Court of the Archdeacon of Bedford. He now showed himself to be Bunyan's implacable enemy. A Victorian biographer of Bunyan, Canon Venables of Lincoln, describes Foster as having 'damned himself to eternal infamy by the bitter zeal he showed in hunting down Dissenters, inflicting exorbitant fines, and breaking into their houses and distraining their goods, maltreating their wives and daughters, and haling the offenders to prison.' Bigoted to an extreme in the cause of Conformity, Foster welcomed the new order and acted without delay. Bunyan was an immediate target. A contemporary biographer recorded that he was again placed at the mercy of his enemies, 'who struck at him forthwith'.

A warrant for his arrest was issued and signed by no less than thirteen magistrates, clear evidence of the desire of those in authority to get him back to prison, for life if need be. The warrant stated that 'many times in contempt of His Majesty's good laws' Bunyan had 'preached or teached at a Conventicle Meeting or Assembly under color or pretense of exercise of Religion, in other manner than according to the Liturgy or Practice of the Church of England'. Scorn and contempt for 'the tinker' were implicit in the words of the warrant. For a third time Bunyan was sent to prison.

It is terrible now to contemplate the bigotry and intolerance shown towards the Dissenters who simply wanted to worship God spontaneously, from the heart of each individual, directed only by the Holy Spirit and the Scriptures. Their steadfastness and courage in facing the cruelty and dangers of those days have become a matter of history. Their bravery helped to obtain the freedoms we enjoy today. Nevertheless it must be remembered that there were many devout and loyal members of the Church of England not, perhaps so theologically aware as the Puritans, but sincere in believing that their patterns of worship were better guided by a liturgy than by being allowed to develop in a random fashion. Each side was deeply suspicious of the other. Though they each dreaded another civil war, their lack of understanding was so great that it was impossible to heal the rift between them.

It has always been a matter of speculation as to which prison Bunyan was taken when he was arrested yet again. Most authorities today, and notably Professor Sharrock, believe it was once more the County Gaol. But for generations after his lifetime there was a very firm and unbroken tradition that he spent the next six months imprisoned in the little Town Gaol on Bedford Bridge. One reason for this was the local name for the Town Gaol—it was called 'The Den' in those days. Now Bunyan begins *The Pilgrim's Progress* with these words: 'As I walked through the wilderness of this world I lighted upon a certain place where there was a Den, and I laid me down in that place to sleep; and as I slept I dreamed a dream.' In the third edition of *The Pilgrim's Progress* Bunyan had the explanatory words 'The Jail', printed in the margin beside these words.

His contemporary biographer states, 'They put him into prison a third time, but that proved but for about half a year.' It is extemely likely that during this time he continued writing, and finished *The Pilgrim's Progress*. ✓ This is suggested by a small puzzle in the book. Some way through *The Pilgrim's Progress* these words occur for no apparent reason: 'Then I awoke and dreamed again.' This rather suggests that there was a break in the narrative, and that at some later date he took up his pen again and decided to continue the writing. Perhaps in 1672 when he was freed after twelve years, he became so wholly occupied with his work as pastor of the Bedford Meeting and with building up the many churches and meetings in a large area around, that he put that particular writing aside. He also had to work hard to support his wife and large family, particularly when there was a new baby. He must have had, one imagines, to train Thomas and John so that they could help him build up once more his brazier's business.

Whatever occurred, there seems little doubt that it was in this new period of enforced inactivity that he tried to shut out the squalor of his surroundings and enter a new world of his own through his writing. This is confirmed by the fact that *The Pilgrim's Progress* was first published in 1678, for he normally had his books published quite speedily after they were finished. His own verse 'Apology' introducing the book also suggests it was written in prison:

> Neither did I but vacant seasons spend
> In this my scribble, nor did I intend
> But to divert myself in doing this,
> From worser thoughts which make me do amiss.

Probably it gave him greater pleasure to write this book than any of his other books:

> Thus I set pen to paper with delight,
> And quickly had my thoughts in black and white.

Bunyan could write with spontaneity and swiftness because he was telling his own story in symbol and allegory. He put in picture form much of what had actually happened in his mind as he had faced the giants of doubt, despair, loneliness and fear. There was so much material in his mind, so many memories to retrieve. He had so much he wanted to say as he recalled his own pilgrimage, and remembered the many trials and dangers and times of testing he had faced, as he thought of how he had at last come to unshakeable faith in Christ, to whom he had committed his whole life, and now his prison life, and perhaps most especially that. The book bears the stamp of a 'prison' book. It has an urgency that suggests it was written with a driving purpose. As he wrote on, scenes flashed before his eyes, and characters familiar in his own life peopled his mind with such vitality that they seemed almost more real than his surroundings.

What John Bunyan wrote was more relevant and more immediate to his readers, because he used the language of ordinary people, with its homely expressions and its colloquialisms, and its simple direct prose. But the book's extra quality, its particular mastery of language, came from his constant intense study of the Bible, whose words rang and thundered in his mind and often invested his sentences with the splendour of poetry.

The central character is the pilgrim, Christian, who leaves his home and family and city, which is threatened by destruction. Although mocked at by friends and neighbours, and thought by his exasperated family to have 'a frenzy distemper', he sets out on his great journey, and will not be turned back by all the temptations, difficulties, dangers and disasters that he encounters. Ever and again he is given glimpses of the glory to come in the Heavenly City to which he is travelling. It is the story of a human soul, convicted of sin, desperately searching for salvation, and in mortal fear of being cast out eternally from God's presence. When he at last loses his great burden of sin at the foot of the cross, his joy is indescribable, and he journeys on with a mighty vision of seeing his Lord at last in the Heavenly City.

The book is full of people he knew but in many cases they are timeless, for human nature does not change. He draws their portraits sharply and boldly. Sometimes the villainous characters stand out in the brightest colours; but all are vivid, and at times are so real that they almost seem to walk out of the page into the room.

Mr Worldly Wiseman with his specious advice and patronizing air reveals himself clearly in his first few words to Christian: 'Here now, good fellow, whither away after this burdened manner?'

Talkative, who loved above all things to hear himself speak, and appeared outwardly so friendly, 'was a tall man, and something more comely at a distance than at hand.'

Lord Hategood at Faithful's trial in the town of Vanity Fair is a picture of the judge at Bunyan's own trial, Mr Justice Keeling. His character is revealed in his contemptuous and insincere attitude to poor Faithful: 'Sirrah, sirrah, thou deservest to live no longer, but to be slain immediately upon the place; yet that all men may see our gentleness towards thee, let us hear what thou hast to say.' It is to no avail and Faithful meets his death.

The gentle courteous women at the House Beautiful, 'built by the Lord of the Hill to entertain pilgrims in', provide a grave and beautiful welcome for the anxious Christian. However they question him pointedly as to why he has not brought his wife and children on his journey.

Charity: But you should have talked to them, and have endeavoured to have shown them the danger of being behind.

Christian: So I did, and I told them also what God had shown me of the destruction of our City; but I seemed to them as one that mocked, and they believed me not.

Charity: And did you pray to God that he would bless your counsel to them?

Christian: Yes, and that with much affection; for you must think that my wife and poor children were very dear unto me.

Here it is possible to see a picture of Bunyan's feelings to his first wife and little children; clearly he realized that his time of mental distress as he searched so desperately for salvation seemed a sort of madness to his wife; yet through it all he felt very strong love towards her and his 'sweet babes' and wanted them to follow him on his journey as they grew up.

Not only the characters but the scenery of *The Pilgrim's Progress* is taken from Bunyan's real world, from the countryside through which he had tramped and ridden so constantly in his work as a brazier and as a preacher. Here is the flat Bedfordshire countryside with its green meadows through which the pleasant river Ouse flows. Vanity Fair is probably a picture of the great annual fair at Stourbridge near Cambridge, with its streets of booths, its foreign merchandise, its shows, its juggling, the games and plays, the country and town folk, mingling in huge crowds, and the rogues and villains who always haunted such places.

As Christian journeys, he has to face desperate difficulties and dangers: the Slough of Despond—a picture of the deep mud lying in some places on the rough Bedfordshire country roads—where he gets 'greviously bedaubed with dirt', which, like sin itself, clings to him; the Hill Difficulty; the Lions which he does not know are chained; the terrible monster Appollyon with whom he has a fearful and near-fatal fight, in the Valley of Humiliation; the darkness and dreadful terrors of the Valley of the Shadow of Death where one of the wicked ones whispers thoughts of blasphemy into his ear. These are all drawn from Bunyan's own bitter experiences.

When, after many terrible dangers, and some respite in the beautiful Land of Beulah, Christian and his companion and true friend Hopeful arrive at last at the deep dark river which had no bridge, and had to be crossed by all pilgrims, there is a most poignant picture of Christian's final torment of fear that he would sink and be lost in the river. Bunyan always depicts Christian as a man of 'like fears' as himself. He is vulnerable and fearful as so many truly are at heart. But he utterly refuses to be turned back, even when he feels he might die on his great journey. And therein lies his courage. At the brink of the river, Hopeful, always looking forward, steadfastly supports Christian in the dark water, and at times half carries him across:

> Christian began to sink, and crying out to his good friend Hopeful, he said, 'I sink in deep waters, the billows go over my head, all his waves go over me.'
> Then said the other, 'Be of good cheer, my brother, I feel the bottom, and it is good.'...A great darkness and horror fell upon Christian, so that he could not see before him.

At last Hopeful, who had great difficulty in holding Christian's head above the water, cries out,

> 'Brother, I see the Gate, and men standing by to receive us.' But Christian would answer, ''Tis you, 'tis you they wait for, you have been Hopeful ever since I knew you.'

Hopeful reminds Christian that his troubles and distress are only sent to prove whether he will 'live upon' or trust the Lord of the City throughout them. He says: 'Be of good cheer, Jesus Christ maketh thee whole.' With that, Christian suddenly calls out with a loud voice:

> 'Oh, I see him again! And he tells me, When thou passest through the waters, I will be with thee, and through the rivers, they shall not overflow thee.' Then they both took courage, and the enemy was after that as still as a stone, until they were both gone over.

There then comes the moment of pure and utter joy as the pilgrims are welcomed by the angelic host. Bunyan is here so deep in his story, so wrapt in his vision of glory, that he is transported to heaven itself, and he must have wept as he, the poor prisoner, wrote these words describing Christian and Faithful's entry into the Heavenly City:

They were transfigured, and they had raiment put on them
that shone like gold... Then I heard in my dream, that all
the bells in the City rang again for joy; and that it was said
unto them 'Enter ye into the joy of your Lord.'

As he wrote he was surely overcome with the beauty
he had created. But he knew the story had to end in the
real world. The Dreamer had to awake. Cold reality had
to return. As Bunyan finished his story, the music of
the bells still rang in his head, and his heart held a
longing that would not yet be fulfilled:

And after that, they shut up the Gates which, when I had
seen, I wished myself among them.

John Bunyan, in the Den, had, unknown to himself,
written a great and timeless masterpiece, a wonderful
story which would appeal not only to the mind, but to
the soul, and would inspire men and women for generations to come.

---

[1] In the Bunyan Museum, housed in the church buildings of Bedford
Meeting House, nearly 200 translations of *The Pilgrim's Progress* can
be seen.

CHAPTER 15

The Pilgrim

At last Bunyan was released and was to be free, although never out of danger, from that time on. It seems that he came out of prison largely through the influence of the great Oxford theologian, Dr John Owen, Dean of Christ Church, Oxford, and Vice-Chancellor of the University from 1652-1658. He had also been Cromwell's noted Chaplain. Owen had seen and appreciated the genius in Bunyan, and had become a good friend to him, going to hear him preach when he could. He, too, had endured a short term of imprisonment during the Restoration, but he was a man of great learning, and seems to have been one of the very few who could in any way bridge the gap between the Establishment and Dissenters. He was once asked by Charles II how he, such a learned man, could go and listen to the preaching of an illiterate tinker. Owen answered, 'May it please your Majesty, could I possess that tinker's abilities for preaching, I would most gladly relinquish all my learning.'

After the Restoration he is known to have remained on friendly terms with Bishop Barlow of Lincoln who had been his tutor at Oxford. Bedford was then in the Diocese of Lincoln, and Owen certainly spoke with Barlow and asked his help in obtaining Bunyan's release. However, it is thought that it was mainly the influence of Owen himself which finally secured it. Eventually Owen became a very noted Nonconformist preacher at his meeting-house in White's Alley, Moorfields, in London. Here many titled people came to hear him, as well as city merchants, and many other people in leading walks of life.

Owen was a writer of many theological works and his publisher was a certain Nathaniel Ponder who published in London at The Sign of the Peacock, in the Poultry. He himself had also been imprisoned as a Dissenter, but was free again when Bunyan came out of prison. He was described by a contemporary as a man who had 'sweetness and enterprise in his air'. It seems very probable that Bunyan, asking advice about the publishing of his new book, *The Pilgrim's Progress,* was advised by Owen to go to Ponder.

In 1678, Nathaniel Ponder published the first edition of *The Pilgrim's Progress* in a little octave volume of 232 pages, for eighteen pence. It caused a stir, and immediately became immensely popular, seizing the imagination of a great public. Two more editions followed within a year, and so great was the popularity of the book that Ponder became known everywhere as 'Bunyan' Ponder. Edition followed edition. Bunyan had given the world his finest sermon of all time, a story in allegory and myth that combined great spiritual vision, rich and glowing imagination, and an exciting drama crowded with familiar human characters. It was a book which was eventually to cross barriers, to inspire people of all ages and outlooks, and to create greater understanding and greater sympathy for the Puritans.

Although it is impossible to give any full account of Bunyan's last years, small pictures of his life and character can be found in a few contemporary writings, in Records of the Bedford Meeting, some written in his own hand, and in his own books which afford hints and suggestions about his thoughts and outlook. All these have to be pieced together like a jigsaw, and the search for the truth is fascinating.

From the Bedford Meeting Book it is clear that Bunyan had become tolerant, open and loving towards all true and sincere Christians. One entry which certainly implies this, concerns a letter of commendation written to another Church or Meeting on behalf of a certain Samuel Hensman who was moving to their district. This writing of 'Letters of Commendation' followed a biblical pattern, alluded to in the New Testament epistles. Such a letter opened the way for a Christian welcome to members of one Meeting who moved as strangers to another place, or were even just visiting. It is interesting to note that the many evangelical meetings of the Christian Brethren, who are among the spiritual descendants of the Puritans, still carry out this practice today. The letter written during Bunyan's pastorate to the gathering of Christians meeting at Braintree asked that Samuel Hensman 'be received by you in the Lord' and 'nourished in the church'. It went on, 'Because as we are informed concerning you beloved, you are not rigid in your principles, but are for communion with saints as saints; and have been taught by the Word to receive the brotherhood because they are beloved and received of the Son to whose grace we commend you.'

Bunyan, in fact, had the utmost charity to those who differed from him, and, as a contemporary commented about him, he had no rigid sectarian outlook. Wherever he found true Christian faith and love, he regarded external differences as not important. 'I would be, as I hope I am, a Christian,' he said, and went on to say that he regarded all the 'factious titles', such as Anabaptist, Independent and Presbyterian and others as coming from 'Hell or Babylon'. An early contemporary biographer wrote of him:

> He was a true lover of all that love our Lord Jesus, and did often bewail the different and distinguishing appellations that are among the godly, saying he did believe a time would come when they should all be buried.

He was, in fact, a forerunner of those who consider themselves 'all one in Christ Jesus'.

It is interesting that there was no strict rule about baptism in the Bedford Meeting. It seemed as if it was left to the will and conscience of members. But the Holy Communion was central in importance. A friend of Bunyan's observed that often when he was celebrating at the Lord's Table, he used to weep as he thought of Christ's terrible suffering on the cross for lost sinners, of whom, like Paul, he counted himself the chief. Joyfully redeemed, forgiven and accepted as he knew he was, the memory of the years of his life he considered wasted by sin never left him. That was why he was, in the words of his friend and fellow-prisoner John Nelson, 'A son of consolation to the broken-hearted, yet a son of thunder to secure and dead sinners.'

John Nelson gives a further description of his work as the pastor, the loved 'Bishop Bunyan':

> As a minister of Christ he was laborious in his preaching, diligent in his preparation for it, and faithful in dispensing the Word, not sparing reproof whether in the pulpit or no, yet ready to succour the tempted...His memory was tenacious, it being customary with him to commit his sermons to writing after he had preached them. A rich annointing of the Spirit was upon him, yet this great saint was always in his own eyes the chiefest of sinners and the least of saints.

He was indefatigable as a pastor, travelling far and wide, but chiefly concerned with his own meeting at Bedford, where he had lived so long, in prison and out. He was asked to go and be a pastor in London, but he refused, as he refused all suggestions of any sort of honour or public position, preferring to be with his own loved people.

Sometimes his preaching journeys were taken at great risk, for feelings against the Dissenters still ran high, and many were imprisoned from time to time. They often had to meet in secret places. One was in a large dell in a wood near Hitchen, to which Bunyan travelled regularly to preach. Before and during the meetings scouts had to be placed on every side to watch out for informers and spies who would do their utmost to get the Puritans arrested. This place was called 'Bunyan's Dell' for years after.

He visited Reading to preach at times. The sense of humour that we see in *The Pilgrim's Progress* reveals itself on these preaching journeys. We are told that in order to travel safely he disguised himself as a waggoner or carter and we can imagine with what amusement he dressed himself for the journey, waving goodbye to his children with his long whip.

As a preacher his fame grew greatly. Charles Doe, the comb-maker, of London, who wrote an account of the later years of Bunyan's life, decided to go and hear him round about 1685-1686. This was when Bunyan had come out of prison for the third time, and there was a great 'storm' against the Nonconformists. Doe's account of the effect Bunyan's sermon had on him is vivid and spontaneous, and unique in coming from one who listened to him at first with some reserve and then came under the spell of his preaching:

It was at this time of persecution I heard that Mr Bunyan came to London sometimes and preached; and because of his fame, and I having read some of his books, I had a mind to hear him. And accordingly I did at Mr More's meeting in a private house; and the text was, 'The fears of the wicked shall come upon him but the desires of the righteous shall be granted.' But I was offended at the text, because not a New Testament one, for then I was very jealous of being cheated by men's sophisticating of scripture to serve their turn or opinion, I being then come into New Testament light in the love of God and the promises, having had enough for the present of the historical and doing for favour in the Old Testament. But Mr Bunyan went on, and preached so New Testament-like that he made me admire, and weep for joy, and give him my affections. And he was the first man that ever I heard preach to my unenlightened understanding and experience, for methought all his sermons were preached to my condition, and had apt similitudes, being full of the love of God, and the manner of its secret working upon the soul, and of the soul under the sense of it, that I could weep for joy most part of his sermons: and so, by a letter I introduced myself into his acquaintance, and, indeed, I have not since met with a man I liked so well.

Later on Doe describes the effect of Bunyan's increasing fame as a preacher, and the way people were drawn in vast crowds to hear him.

When Mr Bunyan preached in London, if there were but one day's notice given, there would be more people come together to hear him preach than the meeting-house would hold. I have seen to hear him preach, by my computation, about twelve hundred at a morning lecture, by seven o'clock, on a working day, in the dark winter time. I also computed about three thousand that came to hear him one Lord's Day, at London, at a town's end meeting-house, so that half were fain to go back again for want of room, and then himself was fain, at a back door, to be pulled almost over people to get to his pulpit.

This period of preaching most likely occurred after the death of Charles II, who had a sudden and fatal seizure in 1685, when for a short time there was greater freedom for the Nonconformists. By now, John Bunyan was increasingly aware of the power of his preaching and necessity to continue with unceasing zeal. Yet he also knew that there was a danger in it, quite apart from the physical dangers of arrest. It was summed up in a story told by a friend. One day he had preached 'with peculiar warmth and enlargement', and one of his hearers remarked to him 'what a sweet sermon' he had preached. We can imagine Bunyan looking penetratingly at the speaker as with dry humour he answered, 'Aye, you have no need to tell me that, for the devil whispered it to me before I was well out of the pulpit.' The danger he saw was that of pride, but he would have said that in all he did, he only wanted to glorify the Lord Jesus.

Indefatigable as he was in his preaching, he still continued ceaselessly to write. It is as if he just could not cram enough into his life to witness to his Lord. His pleasure at the reception given to *The Pilgrim's Progress* was obviously very keen, and it must have astonished him when his book was translated into other languages, and was published and welcomed in America (New England), and in many places across the world. With an almost naïve delight he expresses his pleasure about this in the verse Introduction to its sequel, the Second Part of *The Pilgrim's Progress,* written under far happier conditions when he was a free man:

> In France and Flanders where men kill each other
> My pilgrim is esteemed a friend, a brother.
> In Holland too, 'tis said, as I am told,
> My pilgrim is with some worth more than gold.
> Highlanders and wild Irish can agree,
> My pilgrim should familiar with them be.
> 'Tis in New England under such advance,
> Receives there so much loving countenance,
>   As to be trimmed, new clothed and decked with gems,
> That it might show its features, and its limbs,
> Yet more; so comely doth my pilgrim walk,
> That of him thousands daily sing and talk.

The years after the publication of *The Pilgrim's Progress* were to be some of Bunyan's happiest. His mind, which had been so tortured with doubts and despair until his conversion, was at peace; his faith was strong, serene and confident; the success of his writing and his growing popularity and indeed fame as a preacher filled him with pleasure. He now had certain influential friends, one being Dr John Owen and another a Lord Mayor of London, Sir John Shorter. The latter gave him a silver and ivory handled walking-stick, no doubt in appreciation of Bunyan's work; and Bunyan was called by some his 'teacher', so Sir John must have gone to listen to him at some of the Nonconformist meeting-houses in London when he went to preach.

His anxiety for his 'sweet babes', so acute when he was separated from them in prison, was over, for they were by now grown-up except for his youngest son Joseph. Records show that Bunyan's daughter, Elizabeth, by his first wife, was married; Thomas had also married, but his first wife died leaving him a little son of two years old; and certainly one can imagine that Bunyan's loyal and loving wife Elizabeth would care for the tiny boy. Sarah, Elizabeth's own daughter, was to be married in 1686. His beloved blind Mary died some time in the 1680s.

But in spite of this period of comparative peace, Bunyan never felt free from danger, nor from sudden attack or even arrest. There was still discontent and confusion in England. In the long aftermath of Civil War, Dissenters met with cruelty and constant harassment. Conflict was continued through the rise to prominence in Parliament of the Whigs and Tories, who roughly corresponded in outlook to the Roundheads and Cavaliers respectively.

Bunyan, who had known all too well Elizabeth's plight and destitution when he first went to prison, took steps to provide for his wife by making a Deed of Gift, by which he left all his worldly goods to her. In his own handwriting, the Deed stated that, for 'the natural affection and love which I have and bear unto my well-beloved wife, Elizabeth Bunyan', he gave to her 'all and singular my goods, chattels, debts, ready money, plate, rings, household stuff, apparel, utensils, brass, pewter, bedding, and all other my substance whatsoever.'

A seal was fixed to the deed and also a silver twopenny-piece. It was then hidden so well in a recess in his house in St Cuthbert Street that in after years even Elizabeth did not know where it was, and it was not discovered until two centuries later. In this document Bunyan still calls himself 'brazier', so that it seems likely that his business continued throughout his pastorate.

The Deed might well have been needed. When Charles

charles II died his brother James II came to the throne. A stubborn, tactless and revengeful man, he was a Roman Catholic. It was said of him that he never forgot an enemy, and seldom remembered a friend. It was his intention to restore the Roman Catholic Church in England, and he ruthlessly appointed Catholics to many important positions in Church and State. For a time, during the first part of *1685*, 1685, the persecution of the Nonconformists raged with increasing fierceness. Spies were active, magistrates, churchwardens and rectors were alert to report them and have them arrested, and Dissenting ministers dared not walk in the streets in many places.

All through these years, John Bunyan calmly and with untiring energy continued to write. His output was prodigious. He wrote forty more books, including various religious tracts, but his main works were *The Life and Death of Mr Badman,* published in 1680, and *The Holy War* in 1682. Mr Badman depicts the life of a truly evil man, who was clearly meant as the complete contrast to Christian in *The Pilgrim's Progress.* The portraits, a real rogues' gallery, are sharp and cynical. There is keen insight into character and motive, and no doubt in prison Bunyan may well have met the original of some of the people he portrays Bunyan undoubtedly meant it as a massive warning against sin, but as Mr Badman engages in all the possible wickedness Bunyan can think up, the book palls, and never gains the sympathy of the reader, who cannot identify with the characters as in *The Pilgrim's Progress.*

It has been suggested that such an undiluted picture of evil-doing—Badman dies totally unrepentant—may have, in part, depicted certain repressed desires of Bunyan himself. This would have been more likely if it had been written in his early years, when he did feel strongly tempted to do wrong. It is interesting to note how the media today like to decry Puritanism, on the grounds that it breeds enormous repressions, guilt complexes and inner conflicts. Yet what people outside Puritanism—who have never experienced it as a way of life—seem quite unable wholly to understand, is its happy and attractive side, and the true joy and steadfast courage of many within its ranks, from Bunyan's time to this day. The Puritans found enormous joy and excitement in their faith, which convinced them of their value as individuals, gave them the confidence of being a loved and redeemed people, made them view women highly, and gave them an unbreakable hope and expectation of the life to come. The strict disciplines, the rules of behaviour, the simple dress, were quite secondary to this, and at best were the outward signs of an inner spirituality.

In the remarkable account of her life, previously referred to, the young Puritan, Agnes Beaumont, refers constantly to what might be termed her 'joy in the Lord'. This was obviously a very deeply felt experience. There was nowhere, she said, in the house or farm where she did not pour out her soul to God in her time of trouble. She felt what she called a heavenly consolation and presence in the terrible moments when she was accused of her father's death. She was sustained and calmed, and was able to bear witness to divine intervention on her behalf.

Of course it may be the case that Bunyan—who certainly had something of an actor's qualities in his ability to draw people to him in his preaching, and to move the hearts of crowds by his eloquence—also had an actor's ability to get 'under the skin' of many of his characters, good and bad, just as a saint or a villain can be portrayed with great realism on the stage by the same man. So Bunyan could be called 'worldly' in the sense of having a real understanding of all sorts and conditions of people, good and bad, and 'Mr Badman' may be one aspect of this.

His second great allegory was *The Holy War*, published in 1682, and it has been said that if *The Pilgrim's Progress* had never been written, this would have been considered one of the greatest allegories in English literature. Certainly Bunyan seems to enjoy himself in this account of the war made by Shaddai (God) upon Diabolus (the Devil), to regain the Metropolis of the World. It is military in its theme, as the army of Prince Emmanuel (Christ) comes to regain the lost town of Mansoul. There are splendid descriptions of armies on the march, and undoubtedly these are based on Bunyan's early experiences in Cromwell's New Model Army. In fact Bunyan, now middle-aged, like so many men through the ages who have fought in the armed forces, is working over old memories, recalling old battles or sieges, and remembering the days when he was a young man, strong and active and caught up in adventure. But now he is trying to turn his recollections to the spiritual profit of others.

The book, a concentrated picture of a battle, reaches its climax when Prince Emmanuel arrives at the gates of the town of Mansoul, beseiges it with his troops, attacks and regains it. There is life, colour and magnificence as the Prince in armour of gold, marches in, his standard before him, and there is great joy in Mansoul. But other perils arise before the final satisfactory ending, when Mansoul is to be transferred into Prince Emmanuel's own country, to be transformed into such strength and glory as was never known before.

The next book that surpasses all these later books is the Second Part of *The Pilgrim's Progress*. The success of the First Part had an intoxicating effect on Bunyan as he records with an almost naive wonder that 'brave gallants', 'young ladies', 'gentlewomen' and children too, all love his pilgrim. Now he turns his attention to Christian's wife, Christiana. One could imagine that he wrote the book especially for his wife Elizabeth and the family. The book is written in a happy and far more relaxed mood than the First Part. The Dreamer falls asleep in a pleasant wood and is no longer in a Den, or prison.

The story concerns the journey of Christiana and her friend Mercy and four children to follow Christian to the Heavenly City.

Christiana is deeply sad at the thought of having lost her husband, 'and for that the loving bond of that relation was utterly broken between them'. Distressed and repentant, she realizes that Christian's 'melancholy humours' had not sprung just from foolish fancies, but from his understanding that 'the light of light was given him, by the help of which he has escaped the snares of death'. After a terrible dream, she is visited the next morning by a messenger from the 'Merciful One' who is ready to forgive her and invites her to come into his presence to join Christian, who now ever looks on 'that face that doth minister life to beholders'. Christiana is told to follow Christian's steps, and go to the Wicket Gate, carrying a letter which the messenger gives her from the King. Christiana gathers her children, and tells them to pack up, and set out with her to the Wicket Gate that leads to the Celestial Country, 'That we may see your father and be with him and his companions in peace according to the laws of the land.' The children weep for joy at their mother's decision.

Eventually Christiana and a young friend Mercy and the children set out. Mercy is much moved by Christiana's story, and tells another neighbour, Timorous, that she thinks she 'will walk this sun-shine morning a little way with her to help her on her way'. Mercy secretly longs for salvation, too, and begins to weep, fearing she may not find it. Christiana comforts her by saying that poor Christian mourned for her own hostility in the past, but 'His Lord and ours did gather up his tears and put them into his bottle, and now both I, and thou, and these my sweet babes, are reaping of the fruit and benefit of them.' She tells Mercy that 'they that sow in tears shall reap in joy'.

This second part of *The Pilgrim's Progress* describes a far less desperate journey than Christian's. The pilgrims are welcomed at the House of the Interpreter by those within 'leaping for joy' at their arrival. They are entertained affectionately:

And one smiled, and another smiled, and they all smiled for joy that Christiana was become a pilgrim. They also looked upon the boys, they stroked them over the faces with the hand in token of their kind reception of them: they also carried it lovingly to Mercy, and bid them all welcome into their Master's House.

While this is quite a typical gentle welcome to a Puritan family when visiting old friends, the impression given is that at last Bunyan himself, separated so long from his own large family, was able in the years of writing this book really to enjoy them, and give them the affection that had been so long pent up during his imprisonments.

Bunyan seems particularly happy with his women and children characters. With Elizabeth and two grown-up daughters at home—three if his beloved Mary was still alive—he would have had plenty of opportunity to study women, hear their point of view, join in their anxieties, joys, sorrows and laughter and admire their loyalty. One can imagine him reading the book aloud to blind Mary and others of the family as he wrote it. One of the underlying themes of the book is the loving close relationship between Christiana and Mercy, whose charms are gently described. Was Mercy a picture of one of his daughters? He seems so well able to understand the natural tenderness and love between the two women, that it seems likely.

The book is also a kind of celebration of women. Bunyan shows a natural pleasure in their company, their looks, their talk, their joys. Christiana and Mercy are described as 'a lovely couple'; Mercy is 'alluring'. He sympathetically understands their likes and dislikes. The shepherds at the Delectable Mountains give the women necklaces, and ear-rings and jewels for Christiana's daughters. There is music and dancing. On arrival at the House Beautiful the women hear music, which Christiana says she thinks is for joy that they have arrived. 'Wonderful!' says Mercy. Music in the house, music in the heart, and music also in heaven for joy that we are here.' There are also many welcoming and festive meals for the women at different places on their way. The Puritan in Bunyan is now integrated, and released to become the man who is free to enter wholeheartedly into innocent pleasures.

All this is not surprising when the influence of women on his life is considered: his first wife and her leanings to piety; the poor kind women of Bedford; his second wife's courage and loyalty while he was in prison; her great bravery as she faced his judges; her loving care for his children, and then for her own two; and the sweetness of blind Mary who was so dependent on him yet who brought him soup regularly in his prison.

Perhaps, because it is in so many ways a book about women it is gentler, more leisurely, and in some ways more human. There is time for the marriages of Mercy, and of Christiana's children when they grow up, as the time passes. There is time for talk, stories, and sometimes riddles. Sometimes it all feels more like a picnic than a pilgrimage.

The pilgrims journey on together towards the Heavenly City, passing the same places and the same dangers as Christian. But the perils are lessened by the comforting presence of Mr Great-heart who protects them as they travel. They go up the Hill Difficulty past the lions who now have Giant Grim beside them, whom Great-heart slays; he guards them in the dread Valley of the Shadow of Death where they are 'pale and wan' with its horror; they pass safely by the terrible Giant Despair at Doubting Castle, where, after a great battle, Great-heart, with the four sons of Christiana, now grown-up, slaughter him and his wife, the Giantess.

The final defeat of Giant Despair, whom Bunyan describes as having 'as many lives as a cat', was symbolically very important to Bunyan. His own battles against real despair of mind before his conversion were surely imprinted indelibly on his memory. So it is not surprising

— before his conversion —

that Christiana gives a celebration party after this event, with music and dancing, and some of her own wine.

The journey holds many moments of pure enjoyment. In the Valley of Humiliation Mercy is enraptured by the peace and quiet:

> I think I am as well in this valley as I have been anywhere else in all our journey: the place methinks suits with my spirit. I love to be in such places where there is no rattling with coaches, nor rumblings with wheels.

Surely Bunyan's words here indicate, too, his own love of the freedom and freshness of the countryside as opposed to the crowded, noisy, narrow streets of Bedford. It is in this valley that the pilgrims hear a shepherd boy singing a song which is still quoted and sung today, and is one of the most beautiful small poems Bunyan ever wrote:

> He that is down, needs fear no fall,
> He that is low, no pride:
> He that is humble ever shall
> Have God to be his guide.
>
> I am content with what I have,
> Little be it, or much:
> And, Lord, contentment still I crave,
> Because thou savest such.
>
> Fullness to such a burden is
> That go on pilgrimage:
> Here little, and hereafter bliss,
> Is best from age to age.

Great-heart comments (and it was Bunyan's own deeply-held belief) 'I will dare to say, that this boy lives a merrier life, and wears more of that herb called heart's-ease in his bosom, than he that is clad in silk and velvet.'

As they journey, the pilgrims are joined by others who travel on with them and become dear to them: Old Mr

Honest, who may well be a portrait of a revered senior
member of Bedford Meeting; Mr Valiant-for-Truth, whose
wounds the women wash. He sings the words which have
become ever since the great song of the pilgrim church,
and of a pilgrim people, and are possibly Bunyan's finest
verses:

> Who would true valour see
> Let him come hither;
> One here will constant be,
> Come wind come weather
> There's no discouragement,
> Shall make him once relent,
> His first avowed intent
> To be a pilgrim.
>
> Who so beset him round,
> With dismal stories,
> Do but themselves confound;
> His strength the more is.
> No lion can him fright,
> He'll with a giant fight,
> But he will have a right,
> To be a pilgrim.
>
> Hobgoblin, nor foul fiend,
> Can daunt his spirit;
> He knows, he at the end,
> Shall life inherit.
> Then fancies fly away,
> He'll fear not what men say,
> He'll labour night and day,
> To be a pilgrim.

They meet also Mr Standfast, whom they find thanking
God at having escaped from the wiles of the powerful
Madam Bubble, mistress of the world, who has done all
she can to entice him with 'her body, her purse and her
bed'. Here Bunyan describes the temptation to lust, as
opposed to love. His colourful and lively description of

Madam Bubble who is, 'a tall comely dame, with something of a swarthy complexion' is surely a warning to his own sons and his readers, in a skilfully written and acceptable form, where direct preaching could well misfire.

The book begins to reach its great climax when the long journey is nearly over for Christiana, and she and the pilgrims reach the land of Beulah. The glory is again in Bunyan's eyes as the vision of unutterable beauty unfolds in his imagination. It is a land where 'the sun shineth day and night'; the bells and the trumpets rang out constantly; and a legion of Shining Ones come down to wait for pilgrims to arrive, and to welcome them. The children in Beulah go into the King's gardens and gather nosegays to give 'with much affection' to the pilgrims.

At last the great summons to cross the river comes for Christiana. A Post arrives from the Celestial City telling her that 'The Master calleth for thee'. She summons Mr Great-heart and her children, and blesses them, and then calls for Mr Valiant-for-Truth and asks him to watch over her family and encourage them. She gives a ring to Mr Standfast. Then she goes down into the river, and the last words they hear her say as she enters the deep waters are 'I am come Lord, to be with Thee and bless Thee.' The road is full of people who have come to say farewell and to see her take her journey. On the other side of the river they see a glorious sight of horses and chariots which had come down from above to accompany her and carry her up to the gates of Celestial City.

Soon the summons comes for Mr Ready-to-Halt and Mr Feeble Mind; and after some time for Mr Despondency and his daughter Much-afraid. In some of these pilgrims, so human in their weaknesses, Bunyan no doubt saw traces of himself as well as of many other people. To Mr Ready-to-Halt, 'that good man', who went on crutches, Christiana had said as she prepared to go down to the river, 'Thy travel hither hath been with difficulty, but that will make thy rest the sweeter.' At the river he left his crutches behind, saying that he would have no more need of them.

When at last Mr Valiant-for-Truth 'was taken with a summons', his passing is described in one of the most beautiful passages Bunyan ever wrote. The last to go over the river was Mr Standfast. As Bunyan pictured his passing, it was as if heaven opened to his sight, and words alone could not contain the vision:

> But glorious it was, to see how the open region was filled with horses and chariots, with trumpeters and pipers, with singers, and players on stringed instruments to welcome the pilgrims as they went up and followed one another in at the beautiful Gate of the City.

Four years after he wrote this, in 1688, Bunyan was approached by a young man, a neighbour of his, who had had a quarrel with his father, who threatened to disinherit him. He begged Bunyan to intervene on his behalf, to help bring about some reconciliation between his father and himself. Bunyan, ever ready to act as a peacemaker, and to heal a broken relationship, mounted his horse to make the long ride to Reading to see the father, where his mission was successful. He started to ride back towards London where he was due to preach on the Sunday at a meeting-house near Whitechapel. During his forty mile ride he was caught in torrential rain and was soaked to the skin. He was very weary and beginning to feel unwell when he reached the house of his 'very loving friend', John Strudwick, a grocer and chandler, with whom he was to stay in Snowhill. He managed to fulfil his preaching engagement on the Sunday, August 19th. His sermon, which was totally free from all sectarianism, was an exhortation for Christians to love one another:

> If you are the children of God, live together lovingly. If the world quarrel with you it is no matter; but it is sad if you quarrel together . . . Dost thou see a man that has the image of

God in him? Love him, love him. Say, 'This man and I must go to heaven one day.' Serve one another. Do good for one another. If any wrong you, pray to God to right you, and love the brotherhood.

The following Tuesday he became dangerously ill, and he died of pneumonia ten days later. He was not yet sixty. He never saw the new era of religious liberty that was so soon to open, and for which he had steadfastly fought. As well as his family, the members of the Bedford Meeting were shattered, and wrote poignantly in the Church Book of his 'grievous' death. Their own beloved Mr Great-heart had been taken from them.

Charles Doe, his friend and publisher was, like hundreds of others, extremely distressed. He wrote: 'I was acquainted with him but about three years before he died, and then missed him sorely.'

John Bunyan was buried in Bunhill Fields in City Road, London. His beloved Mary had also died a short time before him, it is thought, and his wife Elizabeth only lived for three or four more years. The fame of the once despised tinker lives on. All others who took part in the great drama of his life are largely forgotten. He had written over sixty books and tracts; he was famed as a powerful and inspired preacher; and he was ever to be remembered for his heroic stand as a prisoner of conscience whose one desire was to witness to his Lord.

There is only one epitaph fitting for him, and he has written it himself. The last words of Mr Valiant-for-Truth before he crossed the river speak better than all others for Bunyan, and for all those men and women of high courage who through the years have shared his pilgrimage:

I am going to my fathers, and though with great difficulty I am got hither, yet now I do not repent me of all the trouble I have been at to arrive where I am. My sword, I give to him that shall succeed me in my pilgrimage, and my courage and skill, to him that can get it. My marks and scars I carry with me, to be a witness for me that I have fought his battles who now will be my rewarder.

Bibliography

Grace Abounding to the Chief of Sinners, by John Bunyan. Edited by Roger Sharrock. (Clarendon Press, 1966.)

The Pilgrim's Progress, by John Bunyan. Edited and with an introduction by Roger Sharrock. (Penguin Books, 1965.)

The Works of John Bunyan. Various editions.

The Pilgrim's Progress with a Life of John Bunyan by Robert Southey. (John Murray, 1830.)

The Trial of John Bunyan and the Persecution of the Puritans. Edited and introduced by Monica Furlong. (The Folio Society.)

Puritan's Progress by Monica Furlong. (Hodder & Stoughton, 1975.)

John Bunyan by C. H. Firth. (The English Association, pamphlet 19.)

Bunyan Calling by M.P. Willcocks. (George Allen and Unwin, 1943.)

John Bunyan, His Life, Times and Work by John Brown, Minister of the Bedford Meeting Church. (Isbister Ltd, 1885.)

Life of Bunyan by Edmund Venables. (Canon of Lincoln, 1888.)

John Bunyan by Gwilym O. Griffith. (Hodder & Stoughton.)

John Bunyan of Bedfordshire by Joyce Godber. (Bedfordshire County Council and County Records Office.)

The Struggler by Charles Doe, a contemporary essay on
Bunyan. (1691.)

Illustrated English Social History Book 2, by G.M. Trevel-
yan. (Pelican.)

A History of Britain by E.H. Carter and R.A.F. Mears.
(Clarendon Press.)

The History of Christianity. A Lion handbook.

A History of the Church in England by J.R.J. Moorman.
(Adam and Charles Black.)

The Select Work of John Bunyan, with a life of the Author
by George Cheever, and an essay on The Pilgrim's
Progress by James Montgomery. (William Collins,
1867.)